BALLET
BEYOND
TRADITION

BALLET BEYOND TRADITION

Anna Paskevska

Routledge
New York • London

Published in 2005 by
Routledge
711 Third Avenue
New York, NY 10017

Published in Great Britain by
Routledge
2 Park Square
Milton Park, Abingdon
Oxfordshire OX1 4RN U.K.

Copyright © 2005 by Routledge

Routledge is an imprint of the Taylor & Francis Group.

Transferred to Digital Printing 2007

Library of Congress Cataloging-in-Publication Data

Paskevska, Anna.
    Ballet beyond tradition / by Anna Paskevska.
        p. cm.
    Includes bibliographical references.
    ISBN 0-415-97017-2 (hb : alk. paper) — ISBN 0-415-97018-0 (pb : alk. paper)
    1. Ballet dancing. 2. Ballet dancers—Training of. I. Title.
    GV1788.P37 2004
    792.8—dc22

                                                                2004014412

CONTENTS

ACKNOWLEDGMENTS

I want to thank my students past and present at the Chicago Academy for the Arts and Columbia College for giving me the daily opportunity to gain new insights into the workings of the technique and to make exciting connections. I also want to recognize the enormous contribution that Maureen Janson and Selene Carter have made to the writing of this book. Maureen read and edited the early drafts and encouraged me to persevere. Selene shared her knowledge in modern techniques and improvisation, suggested readings, and stimulated correlations and conclusions. I would also like to thank Annemari Autere who generously imparted her knowledge of kinesiology, and Nancy Stark Smith who led me to a deeper appreciation of Contact Improvisation. I was at the very beginning of the process of formulating the ideas for this book when we met in Taiwan, and I cherish the memory of our conversations.

Permission to use excerpts from *The Illustrated Dance Technique of José Limón* by Daniel Lewis, copyright © 1994 by Daniel Lewis, has been given by Princeton Book Company, Publishers.

I am also indebted to Ben Dallas who undertook to draw the illustrations and constantly inspires probing conversations into the nature of art.

FOREWORD

Much of what I know about dance I owe to the teaching of Cleo Nordi, who followed the precepts of Nicolai Legat with whom she studied in Russia and in England. Legat's teaching is little known in the States, although Ana Roje has taught his precepts since 1954 in Boston. However, he has a devoted following in England, where John Gregory (a British dancer and teacher) founded the Legat Foundation to preserve his legacy. Nordi often mentioned that Legat did not want his teaching to be labeled a "technique" nor a "method." He taught classical ballet with an understanding of its dynamics and physics avoiding dogma, thus recognizing it as a living, evolving art form. Legat's reluctance to have his teaching labeled a "method" is somewhat echoed by Agrippina Vaganova. As Vera Kostravitskaya noted, Vaganova "never denied the dependence of teaching on contemporary practice and, had she lived today, would have introduced innumerable changes into her system of training" (1978, 16).

As I understand it and strive to impart to my students, Legat's system of educating the body and mind optimizes the body's ability to move and the mind's ability to discover the logic within the motions. This approach acknowledges both the range of motion available to us and the relationship with the space in which we move. Its most salient features are the recognition of gravity's impact on motion and the inclusion of the potential of the spine to spiral expressed in the use of *épaulement*.

When analyzing ballet technique, much is made of the differences among schools—e.g., Vaganova versus Cecchetti, etc.—and there is no doubt that the manner of imparting the technique varies according to one's training. But it is also important to recognize that the technique is an evolving developmental practice and avoid getting mired in dogma from which no method is immune. Dogma, in my view, overtakes a technique when the disciples of the originator teach the method "by the book" without a full appreciation of the reasons for the precepts or a regard for the evolution of dance.

My training experience encompassed several styles. I started dancing with Olga Preobrajenskaya who was greatly influenced by Enrico Cecchetti, although she was a product of the Imperial Russian Ballet and studied with the master rather late in her career. After two years with Preo, I was enrolled at the Paris Opéra School where a generic French style was taught at the time (late 1940s into the early 1950s). However, I continued to attend Preo's classes as well as studying with Serge Peretti and Mme. Rousanne. At age fifteen, I made a short sojourn at the Legat School in England where the teachers ranged in style from old Russian (Lydia Kyasht) to Soviet influenced (Leonid Prowitch). Mme. Legat is generally cited as teaching her husband's system, but when I later studied with Cleo Nordi I realized that my understanding of Legat to that point was rather superficial. My education in classical ballet was concluded at the Royal Ballet School with English-trained teachers and privately with Cleo Nordi.

As an adult, I ventured into modern dance, first at the Graham School with Bertram Ross, then with James May who taught the Limón technique and with Paul Sanasardo. The exposure to modern dance reshaped my understanding of classical ballet and led me to appreciate its underpinnings. It enabled me to recognize the importance of the classical training vocabulary before stylistic differences affected its execution. In other words, my focus shifted from the steps of the vocabulary to the *meaning* of the steps in terms of their impact on our physicality. My teaching is informed by the totality of my experience, however I only gradually introduce Legat's principles to older and more advanced students as his precepts of *épaulement* in particular require a well-established alignment.

Thus, this work does not represent the viewpoint of a unique school, and while greatly influenced by the precepts of Legat, approaches the classical technique from a more general and I hope organic position. In 1981 I wrote *Both Sides of the Mirror* in response to my perception that the students I taught at Indiana University had very little if any idea about the more advanced principles of the classical technique, that is, why they were doing what they were doing and how barre exercises served the vocabulary. Alignment was a quaint notion and *épaulement* was what you did with the head. *Both Sides of the Mirror* was followed by *From the First Plié to Mastery, an Eight Year Course* (1990, reprinted by Routledge in 2002). This time the book was written in response to requests from some colleagues who live and teach in isolated parts of the United States and felt the need for guidance in developing a course of study.

In the past thirty years I have taught students of all ages in a variety of places, have seen a lot of dance, and talked to some extraordinary people in the field. I write this book not only from my personal perspective of these years of exploration, but also from the perspective of the evolution of the dance field. Modern and ballet dancers are no longer on opposite sides of a tall fence. Somatics and idiokinetic techniques are recognized to be relevant to ballet, and a strong technical base is essential for all dancers. Thus I see this book as being in direct line with *Both Sides of the Mirror* in terms of a deepened appreciation of the scope of the classical technique.

I would also like to underscore from the outset that this book is about *technique*, not *style*. Because the body, with its propensity to move, is the instrument of the dancer, style and technique are often confused. Dancers build their instrument through practice and simultaneously acquire a vocabulary of previously unknown motions. Once the musculature has been molded and body/mind connections have become inured, the dancer has acquired the ability to use her/his instrument in many different ways. The application of these skills can be considered style. However, dancers continue to rely on their technical ability to produce the style. In other words, *technique* includes levels of competence, while *style* is the decision to use that competence in specific ways. Aesthetics encompass both technique and style and usually guide in the selection of material to be performed.

The differences between ballet and modern dance is often characterized by the claim that ballet is "up" while modern dance is "down," meaning modern dance works with gravity while ballet defies it. There is an implicit confusion in that statement; it disregards the difference between subjective experience (the *dancer's* experience), with objective experience (the *audience's* experience). No dancer can escape gravity, which includes managing the weight of the body. The dancer either chooses to disguise the effects of gravity, or chooses to reveal them. That is, while the audience sees a sylphan creature hovering miraculously on the tip of a toe, the dancer's experience is wholly other: She is firmly grounded on the floor through that improbable toe, her musculature totally engaged, while a myriad of adjustments are actively counterbalancing to enable her to maintain the pose.

I would suggest that the differences between modern dance and ballet reside primarily in the aesthetic realm and the choreographic field (although in the latter boundaries are often blurred). Moreover, both disciplines have to obey physical laws therefore basic concepts that govern motion, explored in this work, are equally relevant to both disciplines.

Legat urged his students not to copy him but to think for themselves. In that spirit I set out to explore the correlations between modern dance concepts and ballet with a view to enliven our perceptions and thereby the teaching of ballet technique.

1
Moving Beyond Tradition

1

INTRODUCTION

All dance forms use the body as the instrument. All require flexibility, strength, control, awareness of intent and meaning, kinetic energy, and musicality or rhythmic awareness. The body in motion obeys physical laws, thus, moving efficiently through space is dependent upon a recognition and understanding of the forces, both within and without, acting on the body. This work explores ballet technique from the perspective of consciously understanding these forces by analyzing and discussing concepts used in modern dance as they relate to the balletic vocabulary. These concepts offer the opportunity to think of the technique in different terms, to change the words and ideas used to impart the intent of the technique, and to encourage students to perceive movement from a deeper and truer (in terms of the physicality of the technique) perspective.

I have chosen *The Illustrated Technique of José Limón* by Daniel Lewis (1984) as a paradigm of modern dance technique, because the concepts Lewis discusses precede the many applications that have emerged in the postmodern era yet, they remain inevitable features of motion. No matter what style of modern technique is practiced, all address the same basic concerns:

1. Moving from the center
2. Distribution and use of weight and the sister concepts of fall, recovery, and rebound
3. Isolation of parts and the relation of parts to the whole
4. Opposition to create breadth and balance
5. Suspension as it manifests in phrasing

6. Succession to guide in the use of transitions
7. Potential and kinetic energy as they impact dynamics

These terms may not all be part of the lexicon of contemporary choreographers, nevertheless in practice the qualities they suggest are inescapable part of motions. For example, weight, suspension, and opposition are certainly features in Release technique.[1] We can readily recognize the use of potential and kinetic energy in the works of Paul Taylor, Bill T. Jones, or Lucinda Childs, among others. I would further suggest that all dance disciplines share the same concerns and emphasize one or another feature of the human movement potential through the aesthetic they espouse. My aesthetic was formed by the Western theatrical traditions and it is from that foundation that I relate the concepts of modern dance to ballet practice.

Many dancers draw on somatic and body/mind techniques in their training. The term "somatics" can be broadly defined as the body perceived from within, that is, a subjective apprehension of the effect of movement on one's body. In this sense, this book approaches ballet technique from the perspective of a personal experience, but a personal experience that manifests itself within an established aesthetic. There are a plethora of somatic techniques that are available as resources for dancers—including yoga, Pilates, Alexander Technique, Bartenieff Fundamentals, Body Mind Centering™, Feldenkrais, and the work of Irene Dowd and Eric Noel Franklin in Ideokinetics—the concepts underlying the Limón technique are most applicable to my purpose because they deal with *quality of motion* as contrasted with *neuromuscular repatterning*, which concentrates on alignment, freedom of the joints, and flexibility. I am far from dismissing the "mechanics" of motion, as there can be no quality without correct usage of the body, but while I address correct usage, the emphasis of this work is on quality and nuance, and presupposes a thorough knowledge of ballet technique.

While using the Limón definitions for the concepts to be discussed in depth, I will refer to the various somatic approaches and styles that are practiced in modern dance today as they become relevant to the subject. My intention in this choice is to avoid the stylistic differences both in the classical and the modern idioms. It could be said that I aim to deconstruct the forms, and address the usage of the motions in their sparest manifestation.[2]

It is precisely because ballet training is so focused on the practice of a specific physical vocabulary that the quality and dynamics of the movements can be somewhat obscured. In this context, the Limón concepts point the way to reconnect ballet training to a more thoughtful physicality because they address the quality of the gesture yet, when understood as concepts, can be abstracted and even modified from their specific stylistic application, and therefore serve more directly our understanding of ballet technique. These concepts can enhance the experience of learning and of performing ballet; and guide us back to a discovery of the intent of the vocabulary and the physical roots of the movement: These roots are firmly embedded in human movement potential and the way the body interacts with its environment, yet this physical aspect of the classical technique becomes too often buried under a veneer of stylistic idiosyncrasies.

Ballet has been evolving for about three centuries. In that time, it has had the opportunity to develop rules and regulations necessary to support its aesthetic, the use of turn-out foremost among its distinguishing features. Terminology arose out of a need to name the movement performed. Terminology is a shortcut, a system of symbols that facilitates communication. But it can also serve to create distance between the meaning and the physical gesture. In a studio populated by non-French speaking students, ballet terminology loses some of its impact. For example, *fondu* meaning to melt, in no way gives a clue about the actual movement, but instead indicates its mood: melting, yielding, soft with some resilience (like taffy).

Typically, ballet terminology describes the *quality* of a movement and not its *mechanics*. But when the name of the step only conjures up the *shape* and surface muscular manipulation of the body (which is the almost inevitable result of learning by imitation and rote), the dancer performing it is likely to overlook the support of the inner musculature, and the roles gravity and contact with the floor play in motion. Furthermore, the quality, motivation, and underlying dynamics of the movement are obscured rather than illuminated. The dancer performs the movements without comprehending their significance. It could be said that dogma separates us from real experience.

Although modern dance uses some ballet terminology, it has also developed a language of its own. Like the original intention of naming ballet steps to describe a quality of moving, modern dance terminology addresses basic physical responses and also conveys the concept governing motions. In many instances, it abstracts the concept from a particular movement and allows it to serve different applications. For example, both the Graham and Cunningham techniques (among others) utilize the contraction, but the movement itself is quite different in each technique, although both involve the spine. Concepts are sign posts. They point the way back to the source of movement and provide dancers with the means to address the forces underlying specific movements. Concepts guide dancers in the understanding of dynamics, effort, motivation, and the relationship of the body as it occupies and defines the space in which it moves. These concepts are fundamental to human locomotor activities, and as such are relevant to ballet technique as much as to modern dance.

A standard question directed at teachers is "What kind of ballet do you teach?" If the teacher can claim an affiliation with a well-known choreographer or a respected school, their legitimacy is established. The question also suggests that there is a perception of basic differences that distinguish one form of training from another. But, in a conversation at the Royal Ballet School in 1981, Sulamith Messerer, a prominent master from Russia, remarked, "There are no trends in ballet. There is good ballet and bad ballet, that is all." By this statement, Messerer acknowledged the innate wisdom of the technique, and the universality of the precepts that govern its execution. Stylistic differences cannot be denied, but they primarily serve to emphasize the range of application and interpretation possible within the canon of the art form. When the interpretation is in harmony with physical laws, it advances the technique and is "good" ballet; when it does not recognize the principles of motion, the dancer's subjective experience, and thereby execution of the vocabulary is undermined, and it is "bad" ballet.

The evolution of ballet is furthered through time by the imagination and creativity of choreographers. They modify and stretch the prevalent methods to serve their vision in the choreographic field. Their achievements demonstrate how the technique can be used but do not, initially at least, constitute a training method. For example, it would be rather silly to call the movements that Nijinsky used in *L'Après Midi d'un Faune* a technique.

Inasmuch as the role of teachers is to prepare dancers for the field, training methods at higher levels generally keep pace with specific choreographic demands. For example, most major companies have schools where they hone their students in a chosen style. This is necessitated by the fact that in the United States there are no state schools as in Russia, England, or France, where students are trained within a homogeneous aesthetic. Thus, here the focus on a specific style typically occurs after a base technique has been established. Therefore, the initial years of preparation address, or should address, the establishment of basic technical skills that include building the appropriate musculature through the repetition of the vocabulary. In other words, at the early stages, establishing basic technical skills takes precedence over stylistic considerations. (The early stages of training refer to young children as well as college students who experience dance for the first time.) Furthermore, basic skills continue to support dancers' performance even at the most advanced stages.

Within "basic skills," I would include the correct anatomical align-ment that provides the foundation for correct usage of the joints, in-cluding turn-out; and a knowledge and clean execution of the steps and positions of the classical vocabulary as defined by the *danse d'école* (the academic school style of classical ballet first formulated by Beauchamp). This knowledge encompasses the correct placement of the head, and the arms, and the inherent dynamics of individual steps (as well as their usage in *enchaînements*). Keeping in mind Messerer's statement when considering "correctness;" a movement is performed correctly when it is in harmony with the physical laws of motion as they apply to the body.

There are three aspects to dance training:

1. The physics of movement, which relates to human potential for motion and addresses the acquisition of technique.
2. The mechanics of movement, which addresses the acquisition of vocabulary.
3. The aesthetic that shapes the gesture.

In the moment when inside motivation encounters outside forces, the two meld into an inseparable entity, resulting in an intentional and meaningful gesture. This gesture, carried out by the muscles moving the bones, is guided by the mind that understands the concepts and by the brain that controls the motion. The ability to engage in meaningful and intentional gesture presupposes a base vocabulary that is acquired through training.

The ballet class serves many purposes. First, it instills motion patterns and encourages the formation of a musculature that is in harmony with the goals of the broad classical aesthetic, i.e., turn-out and carriage of the upper body. Once the fundamental movements have been integrated, the emphasis shifts to combining steps in ways that challenge the dancer to experience weight adjustments and transference, maximize their po-tential flexibility, and hone their expressiveness, musicality, and phras-ing. We often equate "advanced" with "complex;" thus many steps strung together and performed at a fast tempo are thought to be more "ad-vanced" than fewer steps at a slower tempo. But an advanced execution of the vocabulary *also*, and for me *rather*, manifests in the ability to ad-dress a greater number of details within any step or combination. Thus, a simple combination that allows attention to detail can teach more than a complex one performed sloppily.

For professional dancers, the class affords an opportunity to reconnect with the foundation of their strength and to address any compensation, shortcuts, or idiosyncratic use of the body, that may have arisen in performance of the choreographic repertory. This is not only essential for dancers who are in companies that have an eclectic repertory, but also for those who have a classically based repertory. Contemporary ballet choreography, as well as the eclectic repertoire of many ballet companies, often challenges the limits of our physicality; to meet these demands, dancers may resort to "cheating" on stage, and need to return to an honest execution of the vocabulary when in class to enable them to cheat again, credibly and with aplomb in the next performance! But flippancy aside, returning to correctness is also a return to basic precepts that ensures that the motions are performed from an anatomically correct base, and thus has the added benefit of prolonging life in the dance by keeping the dancer healthy and free of injury. Thus, an advanced class will generally address the same considerations as those covered in an intermediate class.

The goal of this book is to broaden the base from which ballet is taught and to encourage the recognition that the steps of the technique are manifestations of the principles that underlie motion. Furthermore, the aesthetic of ballet is inherently part of the technical aspects of the form, i.e., any position relies on physical factors for the manifestation of the aesthetic quality. Any discussion of movement implicitly includes the physical factors that make it possible, and the aesthetic consideration that guide its execution. The modern dance concepts discussed in this work are abstracted to address the quality inherent in the movements of the classical technique.

Chapter 2 offers a brief historical look at the development of dance from both the choreographic and the training perspectives. Subsequently, the Limón concepts are explored in terms of their relevance to ballet technique. In the third part of this work, the concepts are illustrated by applying them to the practice of the ballet vocabulary within the structure of a class.

This book is written with the dance student and the dance teacher, in studios and at universities, in mind. This includes people who are curious about their craft, want to understand the body better, and who are willing to entertain the idea that all dance denominations share certain fundamental truths, and that dance—not ballet, modern, or other forms—but dance *itself* is the domain in which dancers dwell.

SUGGESTED USES FOR THIS BOOK

There are several considerations that are addressed when giving a class. Although they may appear obvious to most, if not all, of the readers, they nevertheless need to be stated.

First and foremost, the class is about what dancers in that class need to know and practice. Therefore, the teacher is always guided in the practice of movements and combinations, by the actual capability of the dancers in that class to perform these movements without resorting to compensations or short cuts. For example, the teacher will not demand a high extension to second position from a student who has a tenuous grasp of alignment and cannot maintain placement on the supporting side, or give a *petit allegro* combination at a tempo that precludes closing in correct fifth position and maintaining turn-out. At the other end of the scale, the teacher will not impose a "heavy" class, with many repetitions, on dancers who are on stage every night in a performing season. The class may emphasize building strength, acquiring a vocabulary, or be used as a warm up for performance. In each case, the intent of the class will lead in the selection of content and pacing.

The ballet class has a prescribed structure that allows a full experience of the vocabulary at each lesson. This structure encourages the reiteration of specific precepts that govern the execution of the vocabulary, such as alignment, weight transference, opposition, and use of turn-out. The experience of motions at the barre is applied to the understanding of the vocabulary in the center in the *adagio* and *allegro* sections of the class. In other words, this structure provides the opportunity for the students to make connections and understand, initially with some prompting from the teacher, how maintaining alignment at the barre allows for a smooth transition from one position to another in *adagio* in the center, or how closing solidly in fifth position in a *battement tendu* exercise, for example, facilitates the execution of *pirouettes* or fast *petit allegro* combinations.

When I was teaching modern dance to totally raw students at Livingston College, we started class with exercises on the floor. One day a student, Jerome, put his hand up in the middle of the sequence and asked, "Teacher, when are we going to dance?" Jerome's remark made me realize that it is my responsibility to make the exercises relevant to the students in terms of the goals of the technique. However, making it relevant does not require long explanations; a word or a touch at the right moment, an image, stating a connection concisely, will do.

The aesthetic of ballet is fully supported by our physicality; if a movement or combination is awkward to perform or distorts the body, then it is usually also aesthetically incorrect. All motions share an anatomically correct base that includes the placement of the head and the use of arms. Physically, the head is always placed in such a way as to allow the dancer to manage equilibrium. Aesthetically, the head is turned toward the audience to acknowledge their presence and invite them into the dance (Paskevska 1992, 73). The arms are used much in the same way, to insure and enhance equilibrium and to maximize the force needed for *pirouettes* or jumps. The shape of the arms, specifically in 2nd position, engages the musculature of the torso and thus prepares for an integrated execution of all motions. In other instances like, in *adagio*, the positions of the arms define the pose, ensure balance, and foster smooth transitions from one configuration into another; in *allegro*, the use of *port de bras* engages the torso to facilitate the push off the floor and prolongs the illusion of flight.

Finally, the teacher is not a choreographer. While, teachers are certainly creative and inventive in class, our creativity has two masters: the technique whose precepts guide us at all times, and our students whose interests we must serve. Choreographers are probably not as free to make up their own rules of movement as we would like to imagine, although they do not share the teachers' concerns with correctness and technical tenets. For example, Balanchine—wanting his dancers to move quickly—encouraged them not to put their heels down when jumping. While this practice can be justified in terms of Balanchine's choreographic aesthetic, it is not wise in terms of training. Putting the heels down in jumps allows the Achilles tendon to release and is essential for stability; a habitually tense Achilles usually leads to tendonitis. Choreographic concerns are beyond the scope of this work; suffice to say that there are marked differences between the two applications of the technique, and these differences need to be honored.

With these considerations in mind, the following pages are not intended to offer lesson plans. Nor is this a "how to" book; it does not provide a formula to follow or copy. Rather it aims to introduce ideas to be further explored and subsequently integrated in the studio. The examples given are deliberately simple to allow the readers to digest the material easily and apply it in creative ways in their classes.

The teacher may ask: How do I incorporate the concept of opposition into the class? Which exercises lend themselves readily to this application? How does the concept of weight impact on the execution of a *petit allegro enchaînement*? Which steps linked together would best illustrate the idea? These questions provide a starting point; you may then choose to introduce the idea of opposition when giving an *adagio* combination, directing the students' attention toward elongating their line, telling them to extend the gesture/pose beyond their physical boundaries, touching opposing walls with the tips of the fingers or even reaching beyond the walls into space, while the standing leg anchors deeply into the ground like the root of a tree. Or draw their attention to the moment of suspension between an *arabesque* and a *tombé,* which can be both like a breath and a surrender. Or emphasize the use of weight in a fast moving *allegro* combination making them aware of pushing into the floor in order to push off, contrasting jumping in sand to jumping on a springboard. Sometimes it is necessary to explain a movement in mechanical/muscular terms, while other times an analogy, engaging the imagination, works better. The most important aspect of teaching dance is to provide students with a kinetic experience to bring concepts alive and to allow for ownership of the sensation created. (The Class, Chapter 15, is a further guide as to how these concepts manifest themselves in actual practice, but is not intended as a blueprint.)

For the dancers reading these pages, the concepts presented can serve to broaden their base of knowledge of the technique and their own physicality. It can almost become a game to find a concept embedded in a combination, to see how the awareness of the concept impacts on the execution of the step or pose, and enhances the perception of the movements. You could experience how the concept of opposition impacts on balance or the breadth of an *arabesque,* and how the concept of weight allows for greater speed and accuracy. This might be accomplished most easily in the center when the class is divided into groups and you have a moment to reflect on the exercise.

Finally, the book can be used in a theory class where the concepts can be isolated, discussed, and applied to movements of the vocabulary in a format that promotes analysis and debate.

I encourage you, whether studio/university teacher or dancer, to read these pages with an open mind, determine if the concepts discussed can be of use to you in your teaching and dancing, whether they can enhance your apprehension of the technique, and, ultimately, find new ways of applying the ideas discussed.

2

BRIEF HISTORICAL PERSPECTIVE

TECHNIQUE AND CHOREOGRAPHY

In this chapter, we take a brief look at the evolution of classical ballet with particular attention to moments in its history when choreography was either entirely in convergence with training methods or when the two diverged drastically in their aesthetic.

Inasmuch as training is less public than performance, but nevertheless is the bedrock of the art, a distinction needs to be made between the performance of the art or *choreography*, and its training or *technique*. Choreography, today, is not circumscribed by the rules of a specific technique. Choreographers are free to choose the context as well as the vocabulary for their ballets. In this choice, they aim to create an entity, communicate an atmosphere, define characters, explore some dynamics, tell a story, or even take the formal qualities of dance as both the means and the end. Crafting a ballet is similar to cooking a dinner. First, you select the menu: Is it going to be a Cordon Bleu extravaganza or something simple that the whole family will enjoy? All subsequent decisions flow from that initial choice. Thus Balanchine's *Prodigal Son* tells a vivid story while his *Serenade* is abstractly serene, just as Tudor's *Pillar of Fire* has a stronger dramatic quality than the wistful *Lilac Garden*. In each of these ballets, the classical tenets are adapted, subverted, or extolled, depending on the intent of the work.

Moreover, creative, innovative, and inventive choreographers are seldom interested in creating *dancers*; their chief concern is creating *dances*. Choreographers, intent on finding motions that will most expressively carry the meaning of the work, often stretch physical as well as aesthetic boundaries. As an example, we can take Lar Lubovitch's rendition of *Othello* for American Ballet Theatre. In this dramatic work, Lubovitch enlivens and enriches the basically classical vocabulary with positions, lifts, dramatic gesture, and dynamics that are decidedly gleaned from the modern dance vocabulary, melding seamlessly the whole into a powerful narrative. But this aesthetic freedom was not always available to dance makers.

Although it was the favorite pastime of kings, and thereby reflects the grand manner of royal courts, ballet has flourished under egalitarian, totalitarian, and democratic regimes. Dictators, duly elected presidents, and ordinary citizens alike have enjoyed a night at the ballet. It has been a most adaptable art; serving political agendas as well as its own spirit. It is performed and prized in countries across the globe, including those places where a strong indigenous dance culture exists. So it is misleading, at the beginning of the twenty-first century, to define ballet in narrow cultural terms. Yet the aesthetic sets it apart; therefore, we need to address the roots of what we accept today as "classical."

It is popular wisdom to believe that ballet's aesthetic is based in seventeenth-century sensibilities, which in turn took their inspiration from ideals in proportions of the Greco-Roman times. The symmetry of the human body predisposes us to seek that same balance in objects surrounding us. The Greeks found this balance in human and organic nature, where ratios of width to height could be calculated to arrive at the ideal. For example, "the chambers of a nautilus seashell grow in spiraling increasing patterns. . . . The ratio of the size of one unit to that of the following unit is 0.618. . . . The size of any unit divided by the size of the preceding one is 1.618 . . . this measurement is the Greeks' Golden section on which the Golden Rectangle is based" (Zelanski 1988, 193). Architects, then as now, rely on these ratios in designing buildings. While the Greeks sought to remove the emotional content by objectifying proportions, they also recognized that the eye creates its own illusions and adapted their constructions accordingly: "The architects of the Parthenon, therefore used an astonishing series of 'optical refinements' in the proportions of the building to make it *appear* [my italics] perfectly regular and rectangular to the human eye" (Zelanski 1988, 194).

Sculptors, intent on representing the perfect body of gods and goddesses, calculated ideal measurements by the number of times the length of the head was repeated in the rest of the body. Thus, in the fifth century BC, these ideals were set at seven heads to the height, while in the fourth century BC the body became elongated, gaining in elegance at eight heads to the height. To the Greeks, knowing beauty was a celebration of their rationality and the Golden Section formula ensured conformity.

Dance creates its own illusions because human beings, who come in all shapes and sizes, perform it. However, in the court ballets of the sixteenth and seventeenth centuries, physical proportions played a minimal role in reinforcing an aesthetic of balance and harmony, because dance was viewed from above and choreography was defined, not by individual bodies, but as the patterns and configurations made by many bodies.

When dance moved from court to theater in the late seventeenth century, the dance professionals relied on the elegance of the vocabulary of dances of the royal courts for the formulation of appropriate attitudes and steps, but did not hesitate to enliven their performance with vocabulary borrowed from folk dances, and the physical repertoire of Commedia dell'Arte. At that time, the professionalization of ballet and the innovations of the proscenium stage and costuming brought about an emphasis on technique; the legs of female dancers, at least the ankle, thanks to Marie Camargo (Lee 1999, 96), could now be seen, and individual proficiency as well as proportions became a factor in performance.[1] The aesthetic of ballet, based on the ideals of deportment, presentation, and *port de bras* including *épaulement* (the use of the upper body in relation to directions of the legs), was developed, and the physical proportions of dancers were written about and discussed. Turn-out and *épaulement* served two purposes; turn-out at forty-five degrees provided more stability and offered a pleasing view of the legs, *épaulement* (the word is derived from "*épaules*" [shoulders], thus refers to positionings of the upper torso), enhanced the vocabulary by adding variety to the poses and emphasized the natural oppositional use of the body. The technique developed organically from these considerations and simultaneously addressed physicality and aesthetics. Moreover, in the present context, the motions that were practiced (technique) were the same as those that constituted performance. In other words, technique and choreographic style were synonymous.

The Romantic (1830–1859) era brought more innovations. Rounded arms and softly extended legs characterized this era. Ethereality became the hallmark of ballerinas, an effect greatly aided by the use of *pointe,* which added another dimension to the technical vocabulary. Certain aspects of the Romantic style still exert an influence on ballet today. We can ascribe the view that classical ballet is all about lightness to the need of depicting the ballerina as otherworldly, a creature at home in the air as much as on the ground. But air was conquered by long hours of study that ensured strength and stamina. However, during the Romantic era, the practice still focused on repeating combinations of specific steps in the center, and barre work consisted of a fairly short warm up (twenty minutes at most).

After 1850 the center of dance moved from France to Russia. It was during this period that the synthesis of the three leading ballet styles—French, Danish, and Italian—produced what we refer to as the Russian Style. And it is the technical precepts of this synergy that are largely responsible for revitalizing ballet in Europe at the beginning of the twentieth century. Russian dancers were schooled in the French style as early as 1738 when Jean Baptiste Lande established the St. Petersburg Ballet School. Another Frenchman, Charles Didelot, had a great impact on Russian Ballet from 1801 until his death in 1837, by instituting a course of studies that extended by a couple of years the hitherto required training period of two or three years (Lawson 1973, 48). Also, during the late nineteenth century, many Italian ballerinas performed as soloists/guests in Russia, giving the opportunity for Russian dancers to witness and copy the technical virtuosity of the Italian School, additionally, the great Italian master, Enrico Cecchetti, taught at the Maryinsky Imperial Theatre for several years from 1890.

But it is the arrival of Marius Petipa and Christian Johansson (a pupil of Auguste Bournonville, the founder of the Danish School) around 1850 that had the most significant effect on the Russian Ballet (Anderson 1992, 108). With Johansson's teaching the technique acquired the lightness characteristic of the Danish School, building on the established regal French style and the virtuosity of the Italian School. With the added expressiveness of the upper body, a feature of the Russian folk tradition, the technique was poised for its next evolution. And it found its expression in Marius Petipa's ballet.

It is probably to the later works of Petipa that we owe the modern definition of classicism. The overall structure of his ballets—besides telling the story in a sequentially logical way, a legacy of *ballet d'action* of the eighteenth century (Noverre, 1760)—always included a divertissement that featured adapted ethnic dances from various lands. Moreover, the clarity and predictability of the spatial designs spoke to an aesthetic defined and characterized by the need to please and entertain, and harkened back to the seventeenth century ideal of ordered harmony.[2]

Ballet's training methods kept pace with, and served directly, the choreographic aesthetic; Petipa obliged all female dancers, not just the soloists, to be on *pointe* (Lee 1999, 207). The barre work of the Russian School, in contrast to the Danish and Italian traditions, was extended both in time and inclusiveness, and could take up to forty-five minutes to complete, while work in the center, again in contrast to the other two schools, did not follow a set syllabus but allowed more freedom for teachers to apply the technical precepts.

Many factors converged to change choreography at the beginning of the twentieth century; among the most direct were the ideas of Isadora Duncan. Duncan's aesthetic greatly impressed the young Michel Fokine, who became the first choreographer for Serge Diaghilev's Ballets Russes. With this revolutionary company, Diaghilev provided an arena to experiment with structure, content, and vocabulary. As a result, short works in a broad range of styles comprised the repertoire of the Diaghilev Ballets Russes, and offered an alternative to the three or four act ballets of Petipa. Diaghilev's genius resided in his ability not only to bring together talented artists and to provide the opportunity for choreographers to express their ideas, but also his perspicacity in mounting works that engaged the imagination of the audience (Haskell 1968). It is worthy of note that the Ballets Russes innovations had little if any impact on the established Russian School, because its repertoire was not performed in Russia. For the first seasons Diaghilev assembled dancers from the Marynsky and Bolshoi Ballets to perform during their summer vacation, but after 1910 he established the company on a permanent basis and after the 14-18 war moved his headquarters to Monte Carlo. From then until his death, French and English dancers were added to the company as attrition and repertoire demanded. (Many of these dancers "russified" their names. For example, Sydney Healy-Kay became Anton Dolin; Lillian Alicia Marks changed to Alicia Markova.)

Even while adherence to traditional values remained strong in St Petersburg, in Moscow Alexandre Gorsky strove to bring realism and dramatic content into his ballets (Anderson 1992, 111). He had been trained in St. Petersburg and was appointed *premier danseur* and *regisseur* of the Bolshoi Ballet in 1900. He was greatly influenced by André Delsarte and Emile Jacques-Dalcroze and introduced these training methods at the Bolshoi. However, these ideas diverged so much from the ideals of classicism that the Bolshoi teachers feared his experiments would undermine the very base of the balletic training tradition and refused to adopt them.

This episode underlines the common confusion, still prevalent today, that equates training with choreography. In effect, had Gorsky limited his innovations to choreography he would probably have not encountered the resistance of the teachers. By contrast, Diaghilev, while encouraging his choreographers to produce works that broke away from the traditional "classical" format of Petipa's ballets, retained classicists like Enrico Cecchetti and Nicolas Legat as ballet masters; teachers who ensured that the dancers' technique would be maintained. Gorsky was working within an institution that would not allow him to alter the prevailing method of training dancers, while Diaghilev readily recognized the need to keep his dancers' conditioning grounded in classicism. Thus, he implicitly acknowledged that the aesthetics governing training, and those that influence choreography, could diverge without compromising either.

Up to the time of the Ballets Russes experimentations, choreographers used the vocabulary of training in the formulation of their ballets. In other words, the vocabulary practiced in the studio did not differ from that which was performed on stage. Diaghilev's choreographers showed that the aesthetics of choreography could be independent of the aesthetic of training methods even while relying on the proficiency of the classically trained dancers. This is echoed in Michel Fokine's remarkably modern manifesto that stated, "Not to form combinations of ready-made and established dance steps, but to create in each case a new form corresponding to the subject . . ." (Fokine 1914).[3]

Fokine explored how subject matter and characteristics of specific roles affected the movement vocabulary. In *Petrouchka*, for example, only three characters are on *pointe*, the two Street Dancers and the Doll. The movements of the Moor emphasize his brutishness with close-to-the-floor motion, flexed feet, and splayed-out hands. Petrouchka, on the other hand, seems boneless; a rag doll throwing his limbs from side to side, ending in cowering positions with crossed arms and legs. In neither the Moor's nor Petrouchka's variations is there a hint of a classical position. The Doll's vocabulary uses recognizably classical steps, but they are executed in a brittle and superficial manner expressive of her shallow nature. The rest of the cast are residents of the village and are dressed and shod in a manner appropriate to their character. They move naturalistically or rely on ethnic dance moves, as in the dances of the Coachmen and Nursemaids. In other words, choreographic choices were made within a specific context. Dancer/choreographer Vaslav Nijinsky went even further, eschewing all classically based motions in *L'Après Midi d'un Faune* and *Le Sacre du Printemps*. And, his sister, Bronislava Nijinska, placed the women on *pointe* in *Les Noces*, but freely used parallel positions of the legs, turned-in leaps, angular arm positions, and groupings that anticipate the works of Doris Humphrey.

Even from these limited examples, we can deduce that ballet at the beginning of the twentieth century was broadening its base of choreographic expression while training methods remained conservatively traditional. In the repertoire of the Ballets Russes, classically trained dancers were expected to move in ways that contradicted their training, i.e., parallel and even turned-in legs and non-traditional positions of the arms. Diaghilev, in his search for the new and exciting, gave opportunities for his choreographers to experiment and extend the boundaries of classical choreography. In this evolution, classical process was not forgotten, simply adapted. It could be said, that from 1929 (the year of Diaghilev's death and the demise of the original Ballets Russes)— although new ballet companies were formed and established in Europe and North America, and many exciting works were choreographed by a new wave of creators—the radical experimentations of the Diaghilev era were not sustained. And with the rise of modern dance, stylistic boundaries became entrenched.

Early modern dance innovators went further than simply suiting the movement to the context; they both rejected the aesthetic of ballet and deemed the training method as inadequate to their goals. In doing so they explored the basis of movement, developed theories to explain their choices, and a vocabulary to express them. Martha Graham built her technique on the concepts of "Contraction and Release;" Doris Humphrey on "Fall and Recovery." Earlier yet, Isadora Duncan introduced the concept of "Center" upon which all dancers have come to rely. Modern dance choreographers of the next generation tended to emphasize those features of movement that best suited their own needs and mentality, and traded on their ability to create movement that reflected their individuality. Although many limited their innovations to the choreographic field, they also brought to the training vocabulary new movement possibilities to be explored and incorporated. Indeed, many developed exercises to prepare dancers to move within their particular aesthetic.

Paradoxically, this process, instead of creating more distance between modern dance and ballet, eventually brought the two into a greater understanding. From the late 1970s, modern dance and ballet began to be taught within the same program at university dance departments; and choreographers began to freely incorporate motions from both in their works. The inclusion of ballet into university curricula was, in fact, a tacit acknowledgment of the capability of ballet training to enhance the technical skills of dancers.

Merce Cunningham, although "entrenched in a dance-technical idiom" (Banes 1977, 7), inspired—through his theories of chance dance and choreographic practices—the next dance evolution, which came to be called post-modern dance. The post-modernists of the 1960s reacted against the formalism of both ballet and modern dance, and rejected altogether the need for a technical base. They took their inspiration from "natural" movement: "For the post-modern choreographers of the 1960s and '70s, 'natural' movement . . . means action undistorted for theatrical effectiveness, drained of emotional overlay, literary reference, or manipulated timing" (Banes 1977, 17). Besides influencing choreographic themes and treatment, the educational legacy of the post-modern rebellion is the incorporation of improvisation, and Contact Improvisation, into university curricula.

The 1930s not only mark the rise and growth of modern dance, but also the establishment of ballet companies and schools in North America and England. Under the guidance of Enricco Cecchetti, Ninette de Valois established technical tenets for what was to become the British School. However, the Royal Academy of Dancing was already functioning in 1920. It was formed to oversee the training of teachers, and the syllabus was designed, as it were, through consensus. Adeline Genee (Danish School), Edouard Espinosa (French School), Tamara Karsavina (Russian School), Phyllis Bedells (English, studied with Bolm, Cecchetti, and Pavlova) and Philip Richardson (English dance publicist) comprised the first committee that established the syllabus.

In North America, European and Russian émigrés, many of them former members of the Diaghilev Ballet, settled across the land, opening schools, and forming companies. However, unlike in France and England, a national school with defined standards never materialized in the United States. By the early 1940s, Balanchine had established a stronghold on the East Coast, while the Christensen brothers reigned on the West Coast. More recently, several waves of Soviet trained émigrés have introduced the Vaganova style to American dancers.[4] Today, a variety of styles can be found that influence training offered at professional schools affiliated with ballet companies as well as at university dance departments.

Toward the end of the twentieth century, the classical technique, in its continued evolution, became more extreme in its demands and more uniform. This uniformity partially resulted from the extreme athleticism of the additions to the vocabulary, such as in changes to the vocabulary that Baryshnikov introduced. Some of these more demanding movements include the dancer not only turning in the air but also switching legs before landing, or winding down the *pirouette* and ending, balanced, in a high *retiré*. In these technical innovations, there is little margin for error, and the physics of dance are stretched to the utmost. This heightened the expected physical attributes of dancers and their acquired skills. As John Berger put it in another context, dancers were required to "move with the same inevitability as water finds its own level, and consequently they transcend their rhetorical [technical] gesture" (Berger 2001, 49).

Contemporary times are very difficult to categorize. On the one hand, we have companies that have a defined individual style and training philosophies that inculcate it, and on the other hand, we have an extremely fluid practice whereby dancers move from one company to another, often switching styles in the process. Baryshnikov transformed himself into a modern dancer with the White Oak Project, and numerous others started out in classical ballet companies and moved on to modern dance and jazz companies, such as Merce Cunningham and Hubbard Street Dance Company. In addition, choreographers from one discipline often create ballets for companies with a different discipline. The choreographic field has broadened to allow choreographers to work in different genres, such as Ulysses Dove setting a modern dance work for the Alvin Ailey Dance Theatre and a classical ballet for the Swedish Ballet. Companies seek choreographers working in a different genre to set works for their repertoire, such as Laura Dean choreographing for the Joffrey Ballet, or David Parsons and Paul Taylor working with the Houston Ballet. Thus, even while some ballet companies have become narrowly distinguished within a specific style each associated with a specific training method (New York City Ballet, Royal Ballet, among others), the choreographic field has acquired a versatility comparable to the Diaghilev era.

In contrast to the choreographic diversity, teachers' responsibility, now more than ever, is to ensure that the dancer is prepared both in his/her perceptive skills and physical ability to perform motions that are often beyond the strictly classical training tenets. Stylistic exclusions or inclusions, when applied to the process of acquiring technique, tend to obscure the fact that training is initially about building an instrument. This instrument, unlike a piano or a violin, is fashioned out of muscles and sinews, and is characterized by a continued malleability that is shaped and molded in the moment. Stylistic choices, while an inescapable feature of choreography, when applied to training have the property of *narrowing* the technical choices, and in that process impoverish the scope of the dancers' technical potential. The dancer who has built a responsive instrument is capable of responding to a diversity of styles and to cope with choreographic exigencies. Thus, training is more concerned with tradition, the established methods that have endured through time as capable of fashioning the instrument. The ability to notice order and structure leads to knowing the object, and the resultant analysis supports the capability to objectify. Ballet technique in many ways attests to this capability. It demonstrates how formalistic concepts acted upon the evolution of this art form, and continue to determine its ideals—while allowing for divergence.

Although the term "classical" is synonymous in people's mind with ballet, I would like to extend the meaning of classicism to include artists who have achieved total mastery of their idiom and their instrument, and thereby are able to transcend both and offer to the spectator the spirit of the dance. Jan Feager, a tap dancer from St. Louis, brought tears to my eyes when I saw her dance. The subtleties of the relationship between her motions and the nuanced sounds of her taps were exquisitely balanced and blended. Nancy Stark Smith extended my perceptions of what movement can do and where it can transport you by her astounding improvisations. As a child, I saw Kathryn Dunham concerts whenever her company was in Paris. I always came out of the theater in a joyfully ecstatic mood, dancing in the street all the way home. For me, these diverse artists embody the spirit of classicism.

Within this wide-open creative field, it is now, more than ever, incumbent upon teachers to distinguish between stylistic applications and basic precepts; the precepts that have the property of building an instrument capable of responding appropriately to choreographic demands. In that pursuit we need not become intimidated by the onus of tradition; nor dismiss or corrupt it with well-meaning interpretations, but rather venture to question the well-established precepts, find the reason for their durability, use them in our personal development, and to the greater benefit of the art form.

2
The Concepts

3

THE BODY'S CENTER

Although the idea of "center" has for a long time been a feature of various body/mind, practices, e.g., yoga, it was Isadora Duncan who brought the idea to the attention of Western dancers. She located the center at the *solar plexus.* I suspect the reference for her was more spiritual than physical, as she had little interest in kinesiology or physiology. In Duncan's words, "... I would stand quite still, my two hands folded between my breasts, covering the solar plexus ... I was seeking and finally discovered the central spring of all movement, the crater of motor power, the unity from which all diversities of movement are born, the mirror of vision for the creation of the dance ..." (1927, 75).

The solar plexus is located about the level of the twelfth thoracic vertebra (at the level of the last ribs, somewhat below the lower tip of the sternum). This is also the vertebra to which attaches the *psoas,* the *trapezius,* and muscles of the diaphragm. The *psoas* attaches to the side of the twelfth thoracic vertebra and each of the lumbar vertebrae (one to five) passes through the pelvic area where it joins the *iliacus* and inserts into the *femur.* The *psoas* also borders the diaphragm (whose attachments reach the fourth and fifth vertebrae of the lumbar spine), and therefore the *psoas* contractions affect breathing. The *iliopsoas* is a hip flexor and impacts the way we lift our legs. The *trapezius* attaches at the back of the vertebra and moves upwards to the base of the skull, also fanning out to insertions on the shoulder girdle. Thus, the *trapezius* controls the upper torso and affects posture. In terms of locating a central point of control, the twelfth thoracic vertebra, in fact, connects the upper body with the lower limbs. If we think of the body in motion as a web of interconnections, the twelfth thoracic vertebra acquires a preeminent meaning; and we can regard it with the same awe as Isadora when she spoke of the solar plexus.

The center can also be pinpointed structurally to the place where the vertical line of gravity intercepts with the horizontal, which dissects the standing, erect body in half with equal weight above and below the line. In women the center is usually lower than in men, due to the broader/ heavier pelvic area, although it depends more on ratio between length of the torso and girth of the pelvis than on gender. In practice, the structural center can be somewhat lower than the solar plexus but also varies depending on the individual physique. For example, Martha Graham placed it just above the pubic bone and was probably guided by her own physique: a long torso and relatively shorter legs. This influenced her conception of the contraction, which in her technique starts in the lower back or pelvic diaphragm. By contrast, the Cunningham contraction originates a little higher, and although it involves the pelvis, can be felt most strongly above the sacrum. Thus the idea of center, as opposed to the structural location of the center, can be adapted to serve different needs.

The role center plays in motion can be compared to the hub of a bicycle wheel, its spokes connecting to the outer rim. In a model for the human body, the hub, viewed vertically, is the center and the spokes connect respectively with the two shoulder joints, the two hip joints, the base of the skull, and the sacrum. The hip and shoulder joints can also be designated as way stations, somewhat like fuelling posts between the departure and arrival points, and in that sense they become mini centers. The spokes are only effective in maintaining the structure and carrying out the movement intention if their connection to the hub and rim are secure (see Figure 1).

Additionally it is helpful to experience this connection as a dynamic relationship. Energy flows not only outward from the center to the extremities to give power to the gesture, but also inward toward the centers to preserve the integrity of the joints.

When we are aware of working from the center, we ensure that the torso and pelvic area are engaged in all movements in a mutually supportive manner. This deep-seated awareness affects all motions, the intent and quality of the gesture, and, by extension, moving through space.

Intention is central to any artistic expression but it also has a physical component: core muscles contract as intention is formed. Thus, intention always precedes motion; we *intend* to lift the leg, then *initiate* the motion muscularly. The muscles act upon the joints to move the bones; however, the bones are shape makers. Understanding the mechanics, or the need to create the specific shapes, of individual movements is important

Figure 1

in terms of the necessary muscular effort needed to perform the movement. But we arrive at mechanics, so to speak, by the backdoor. First, we see the shape of the position, then we appreciate the path taken to arrive at the position, and from this we deduce the needed participation of the various parts of the body.

For example, if the intention is to perform a *battement tendu devant,* we know that the leg will end in an extension to the front of the body with the toes touching the floor. From the initial fifth position, the thigh begins to open outward and forward, and the toes gradually point until the instep is fully engaged. In order to remain placed over the supporting leg, a weight shift onto that leg is necessary. Further analyses leads us to question at exactly what point and to what extent the weight shifts, which joints are active, and which, although engaged, are passive (energy flows through them)—in short, how the movement is facilitated by the rest of the body. Initially, we nurture these connections by keeping an elongated spine and an aligned pelvis. By engaging the spine and maintaining an upright pelvis, we ensure that the trapezius and the iliopsoas are optimally positioned to do their work. (There is more on this subject in Chapter 4.)

It is easy to confuse the *contraction* of the leg muscles, specifically the quads, with the *action* of lifting the leg. This confusion overlooks the role of the hip flexors and leads to the overdevelopment of the quads. Just as we are able to walk by thinking of walking and not by listing the specific muscle groups that allow us to perform that activity, so with dance movements we must allow the motion its freedom by not over-contracting or gripping a muscle group; this is achieved by practicing the path of the motion and letting the muscles do their work. In a *développé*, for example, all the muscles of the leg that need to be used will be engaged when the starting position of the body is correct; the shape and pathway of the motion are clear, and the appropriate effort is present. The ability to avoid gripping is informed by the knowledge that the muscles of the torso and deep muscles of the hip joint are supporting the motion. Maintaining an elongated spine and an aligned pelvis facili-tates access to the *iliopsoas* and enables us to utilize its function of lifting the leg. The nurturing and eventual reliance on the inner muscular strength created through training makes controlled, intentional move-ment possible.

Before it became necessary for dancers to have high leg extensions, the role of the center could be easily overlooked. As a beginner in ballet in the late 1940s, I never heard my teachers mention the word "center." We were told to stand straight, to keep the shoulders down, and to hold the belly in. How this was to be achieved was never discussed. So, some of us, pulled in the belly, lifted the diaphragm, and stopped breathing in the process! Unhappily, this positioning can still be seen among dancers today.

As with the legs, the arms require an engagement of the musculature without coercive tension. The arms, in addition to their expressive uses, act as stabilizers. They can also be distracters if they are not connected to the center. The muscles of the arms are designed to control the shape of the arms (with some exceptions, like the *biceps*, for example). The upper torso muscles control their raising and lowering (abduction and adduc-tion). When this distinction is recognized, the arms can move without undue tension. (For a thorough discussion of the role of the posterior muscles of the torso, see the ideokinetic work of Irene Dowd, 1981.)

To begin to appreciate the role of the upper torso muscles, we have to become conscious of the weight of the arms by releasing the musculature of the arms themselves, and actually feeling their weight (Franklin 1996, 10). Subsequently, in shaping the arms to the correct classical position by rotating the *humerus* inward and the lower arm outward the role of the arm muscles in maintaining the shape can be isolated from the task of holding them up (see Figure 2; this description is greatly simplified version of upper body musculature, for more detail see Fitt, 1988).

Confusing the separate functions of surface muscles and inner torso muscles leads to an enormous amount of tension to be stored in the joints of the shoulders, elbows, and wrists. This tension causes the joints to lock, precluding fluidity and freedom; the arms become wooden and lack all expressiveness. Locking joints to maintain a position is counter-productive and ultimately harmful. A locked joint is a stuck and unyielding joint; to move an arm or a leg from that base requires excessive muscular effort. Locking the joints also disconnects the limbs from the center, separating the arms from the torso and making the motions appear arbitrary. It is rather like erecting a dam across a river: the water or energy is trapped, prevented from flowing freely. And like the river, which can no longer nourish the lands below the dam, the center can no longer provide the strength and support needed by the limbs.

The location of the center initially helps dancers to achieve connectedness; the next step in developing technique is to learn to manipulate it in order to facilitate motion. This needs a brief explanation: when we rise on half-*pointe*, the structural center also rises farther away from the floor. The increased distance and the smaller support base give us a feeling of insecurity. To overcome this loss of stability, we can visualize sending our energy down, in effect, lowering the center and thereby retaining a

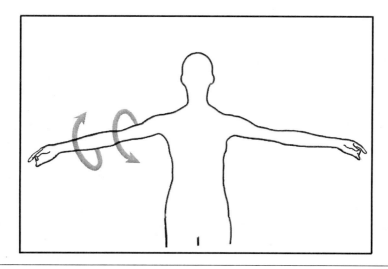

Figure 2

secure anchoring to the floor; we are pushing into the floor, not pulling out of it.

Conversely, in jumps we raise our center to maximize height. Many *grand allegro* steps are performed with arms rising to 5th position, as in *assemblé en tournant, saut de basque en tournant,* or *grand jeté en tournant,* because raising the arms to 5th has the property of raising the center of gravity. The arms rise through 1st position as the dancer pushed off from the floor. They reach 5th at the apex of the jump and remain in 5th through the moment of landing. Maintaining the 5th position until the landing serves both the physical and aesthetic concerns; physically it ensures that the torso remains engaged, and aesthetically it creates the illusion that the dancer is still at the apex of the jump even while in the process of descending. Thus, the technique acknowledges the need to raise the center in order to maximize the push off the floor and facilitates that process by incorporating the arm function.

Each movement of the vocabulary has an optimum form when the arms, legs, head, and torso cooperate to produce a movement with the least effort and maximum effect within the aesthetic line. This is what I understand both *danse d'école* and basic training to mean. Thus, basic training addresses the optimal way to perform the steps of the vocabulary by instilling pathways and connections that provide the means to fully engage the body both physically and dynamically. Primarily, basic training addresses the mechanics of movements. When I give a "basic" correction in class, the response from students is invariably, "Oh, it's so much easier this way!" It is easier because all parts of the body are working toward the same end. Rather like a family engaged in cleaning the house together, each member is fulfilling a specific task.

We can take *emboîtés en tournant* as an example: From a fifth position left leg back, the dancer springs up, bringing the back leg to a low *retiré devant,* with a half turn of the body, the left arm coming to 1st position and the right arm in second (4th *devant*). Then she springs again with another half turn, right leg coming to *retiré,* the right arm to 1st position, and the left arm opening to 2nd (see Figure 3).

Bringing the same arm forward as the working leg and opening the other arm to 2nd, engages the torso to facilitate the half turn. It ensures that the body is squared to itself and that both sides of the body are active (the head spots as in all turns and ensures equilibrium). Bringing the leg to a *retiré devant* engages the thigh and helps maintain turn-out. Once the connections and coordination between arms, legs, head, and torso have been integrated, the dancer performing *emboîtés en tournant* will always execute them with ease, engaging the body fully, regardless of how the choreographer decides to use the arms or place the leg.

Figure 3

Manipulating the center is closely associated with manipulating our weight or mass. We perceive differences through opposites. There can be no "down" without "up," as there can be no "heavy" without "light." In order to achieve the illusion of lightness, we have to bring to consciousness the weight of our body. Again, we are usually less conscious of the weight of the arms than we are of the legs. In extensions, the legs need to be experienced as light; we can achieve this when we maintain alignment and correct weight distribution (weight redistributions occur every time we move from two legs to one). This allows the *iliopsoas* to perform the function for which it is designed (flexion of the hip). It is also through the legs that we maintain contact with the floor, pushing against it to propel ourselves into a jump or to create torque for a *pirouette* (see Chapter 9). Although we are less readily conscious of the actual weight of the arms, their correct positioning and usage provides physical stability and aesthetically enhances all motions. In order to perform both functions, they too must be connected to the center.

Dancing from the center becomes a conscious choice when the dancer is aware of the force gravity exerts upon the body; and of the internal responses to these forces that are manifested in a reorganization around the axis. Any part of the body is perceived more acutely when it is sensed in relation to another part. This is also true for the center. When we appreciate that the muscles of the torso are designed to support the moving of the limbs, then dancing from the center can shift from an abstract idea to become a very real physical experience.

As mentioned earlier, movement not only originates in the center and radiates outward through the limbs, but it is also directed inward toward the axis. This constant flow of energy, both in and out, acts to define motions and adds to the gesture a rhythmic, dynamic, and dramatic quality. These qualities, on the surface, may seem to be more readily related to aesthetics than to technique; however, each is dependent for its expression on the movement used to convey the meaning and therefore has its foundation in technical skill.

Awareness of working from the center builds strong connections between the body's center and the limbs in the initial years of training, by encouraging the development of strength of the torso and the supportive muscular connections around the hip joint. With further study, these connections are refined to provide the dancer with stability, equilibrium, and an ability to move off center when desired.

4

ALIGNMENT

"Ordinarily, alignment refers to the placement of the feet, hips and shoulders in a standing position. But in fact alignment is the placement of *all* parts of the body in relationship to each other" (Lewis 1984, 36). Another useful way of describing alignment involves recognizing the volume of the body. Andrea Olsen describes alignment as, ". . . the three primary body weights, the skull, thorax, and pelvis, organized around a plumb line." (1991, 35).

Alignment creates a body that is in harmony with itself and, thereby, with its environment. The practice of alignment starts by standing erect keeping an elongated spine not unlike the position of a Zen Buddhist as he sits in meditation, "to experience what is immovable in the movable without stopping its movement . . ." (Suzuki 1980, 16). This positioning lengthens the spine, allowing each section of the torso to occupy the space it needs without impinging on another part; that is, each part of the torso is responsible for carrying its own weight. The shoulders can hang from the shoulder girdle without contraction and the ribs slope naturally from their attachments to the spine, allowing the diaphragm to control the breath without impediment. The waist is lengthened by virtue of the elongation between the vertebrae, and thereby this most vulnerable area is supported. Finally the pelvis does not sit into the hip joint, but rather floats atop the joints (see Figure 4). This can be likened to an oil rig in the ocean; the pylons upon which the rig rests reach deep into the ocean floor, while the platform (pelvic area) floats atop the water. Maybe this is what is meant by the statement "ballet defies gravity."

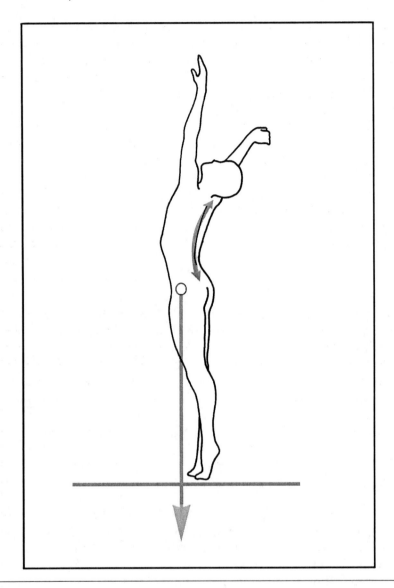

Figure 4

In this respect, even before any motion occurs, by standing upright, elongating the spine, and floating atop the hip joints, the dancer defies gravity.

The elongated stance also has the virtue of protecting the joints of the legs. This is most readily recognized when jumping; the pelvis carries the weight of the torso and the impact of landing is cushioned by the thighs. Thus the impact on the spine, knee, and ankle joints is minimized.

The result of this alignment is a posture that gives dancers a characteristic super-uprightness. It is not to be confused with stiffness, in fact, it is its exact opposite; rather this posture can be described as a *pliable verticality*. Consciously elongating the spine engages the inner musculature, allows mobility in the joints, and predisposes all muscles to respond in an efficient way to the demands of the technique.

To seek the source of good alignment, we must begin with the skeleton. As can be seen in Figure 5a, the line of gravity in an aligned body passes through the center of the body: the ear over shoulder girdle, descending through the third lumbar vertebra, center of the hip joint, center of knee joint, and down to the ankle joint. Figures 5b, c, and d illustrate how even a slight tilting of the pelvis can dramatically affect posture, and most importantly in our present context, cause the line of gravity to shift back. In other words, the farther the line of gravity falls behind the center of the body, the more muscle power is diverted to preserve balance and the outer muscles, working against their own contracted state, have to exert more force to move the body.

It is easy to perceive the spine as being the "knobby projections we feel along our back" (Koch 1997, 17), but as Koch also points out, "What we touch when we run our hands along our backs are the transverse processes, the wing-like protusions of the spine. However, the actual body of the vertebrae sit more forward towards the center or mid-line of the

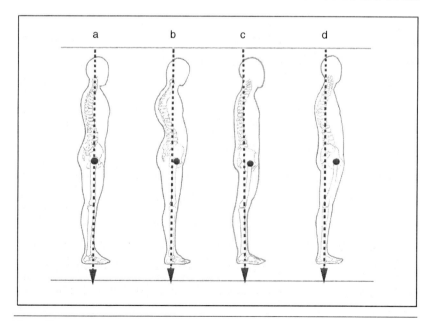

Figure 5

body . . ." We can more correctly apprehend the actuality of the spine when we relate it to our center, like a column of light radiating from deep within. The plumb line is another way of naming the line of gravity.

The principal aim of alignment is to place the body in an optimal position for ease of motion and health. As Mabel Todd noted, "Our concept of good body-alignment should be based first on principles of balance applied to the human body framework" (1953, 123). Principles of alignment address this concern in three ways, through:

1. The internal relationships of the different parts of the body to each other, i.e., head to thorax, thorax to pelvis, pelvis to legs.
2. The relationship of those parts to the axis, i.e., weight reorganization.
3. The relationship of the whole body to gravity, i.e., weight transference.

Gravity tends to pull the body down and back. This force is compounded in backward locomotion because we have no neuromuscular memory for backward motion, and because we are dependant upon our visual orientation to the horizon. The horizon line provides a gauge by which to test our verticality. For example, a dancer who spots (looks up) in *pirouettes* above the horizon line is more likely to fall backward out of the spin than one who spots straight ahead. An exaggerated upright stance or misalignment of the pelvic area that takes us behind the line of gravity also influences our sense of balance.

Loss of balance is always perceived as a threat by our organism, and we automatically contract certain muscle groups in order to preserve equilibrium. As Bonnie Bainbridge Cohen notes, "For every reflex there are opposite and equal reflexes which complement, modulate and resolve it" (1993, 156). In other words, the body is always balancing the forces acting upon it; even in held, balanced poses there is internal movement. This internal movement is characterized by the relationships of the parts to the axis and of the whole to the point of support. For example, in a fifth position on *pointe*, energy through the legs will be directed down into the floor, while from the waist energy is directed up through the spine and into the head; the pelvic area and torso will be gathered around the axis, while the shoulders and diaphragm remain free of tension.

In an aligned standing body, the pelvis is held upright. This positioning requires that the pubic bone be uplifted, creating a connection between the pubis, belly button, and the sternum (see Sweigart 1974, 193), which allows the anterior superior iliac spine to face straight out like a car's headlights, without tilting downward or upward. This positioning releases the tension of the gluteus maximus and frees the hip joint, which permits full access to turn-out. Tucking under—whereby the sitz bones are literally tucked under causing the upper ledge of the pelvis to actually tilt upward—is to be absolutely avoided. This practice creates misalignment all the way up into the neck, locks the hip joint in the acetabular cavity and prevents the free rotation necessary for turn-out. It also encourages an overdevelopment of the quadriceps. Students who are in the habit of tucking under, feel the repositioning of the pelvis as a release of the gluteus, and, as a result, have the impression that their buttocks are sticking out. It is important to reassure them that not only are the buttocks where they need to be, but that—in effect—tucking under *encourages* the development of the powerful gluteus; thus the buttocks will grow larger the longer the student tucks under.

One of my students at Indiana University had a well-developed posterior and was in the habit of tucking under to minimize its size. She struggled to reposition her pelvis and after several months had achieved a better stance and greater freedom of movement. Unfortunately, during the summer, she attended classes at another school where the teachers only saw the big buttocks and not what was underneath. When I saw her again, she had lost the range of motion she had previously achieved, the ability to be truly "on her legs," and she was again struggling with turn-out and equilibrium.

The parallel position provides a broader platform in the sagittal plane than does a fifth position. Therefore, as soon as turn-out is introduced the relationship of body mass to gravity is altered. To compensate for the loss of stability in the sagittal plane, the weight of the body needs to be carried more emphatically forward. This does not mean that one leans forward, rather the inner weight of the body is reorganized and is carried in front of the line of gravity where it can be controlled. One way to awaken the sensation of carrying the weight in front of the line of gravity is for the teacher to place her hands on the student's stomach and belly and ask the student to press into the hands. Through this little device, the student will be led to readjust her weight inwardly and to understand that carrying her weight forward does not necessitate leaning forward.

The placement and relationship of the foot to the floor is another vital area prone to misalignment. In both the parallel and turned out positions, the weight of the body falls on the keystone or the arch of the feet. Although the weight of the body is carried on the keystone, the heels need to be anchored, maintain, or regain contact with the floor whenever the feet are flat on the floor. Contact with the floor is achieved through an even distribution of weight through the metatarsals and the

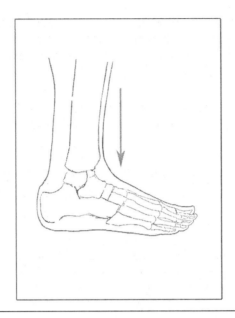

Figure 6

full surface of the heels, to avoid pronation or supination and to pro-
mote a correct alignment of the tibia and fibula in their relationships to
the talus and calcaneus (see Figure 6).

The standard injunctions given in a ballet class urging the students to
"stand straight" and "pull up" are usually misunderstood; students, like
soldiers on the parade ground, hyperextend upward and put the body
mass behind the vertical line of gravity. They then use muscular contractions to keep upright. There is a very high price to pay for this positioning. When trying to move from this unwieldy base, an unnecessary
burden is placed on the body; the muscles cannot respond freely to the
commands given but strain to prevail against their own contracted state.
The immediate result is a strained execution of motions; the long-term
consequence is an overdeveloped musculature. The overdevelopment of
musculature sheathes the joints and impinges on their freedom; the body
becomes muscle-bound.

In contrast to the injunction to stand straight and pull up, consider
Steve Paxton's description of the "small dance" that is used at the beginning of Contact Improvisation workshops to lead students to get in touch
with their core muscles and appreciate the support of this hidden re-
source:

> it's a fairly easy perception: all you have to do is stand up and
> relax—you know—and at a certain point you realize that you've

relaxed everything that you can relax but you're still standing and in that standing is quite a lot of minute movement . . . the skeleton holding you upright even though you're mentally relaxing. Now in that very fact of you ordering yourself to relax and yet continuing to stand—finding that limit to which you could no further relax without falling down, you're put in touch with a basic sustaining effort that goes on constantly in the body (1977–78, 23)

We cannot "feel" the contractions of the deep muscles, the small dance give us an opportunity to connect with our inner strength and perceive the subtle play of gravity. I suggest that this small dance would also be a useful exercise for ballet dancers as a means to become aware of the "basic sustaining effort" and contrast that feeling with the effort they usually expand in simply standing, and learn thereby to modulate their effort.

The barre exercises fulfill the function of centering and aligning the body. Although emphasis is usually placed on the working limb, the role of the supporting side in its response is just as important (see Chapter 6). Maintaining verticality with ease means that the line of gravity is shifted to the supporting side; all the muscles of the torso and pelvis are engaged in that positioning. The barre exercises nurture the ability to shift from two feet to one, laying the pathways by which this shifting occurs. They ensure that the weight of the body is appropriately distributed; and thereby prepare the body to perform the positions and steps of the center vocabulary. This is fostered by a return of weight to both feet when closing in fifth position, laying the pattern for landing from jumps: as the weight descends into the feet, the shock of the impact is cushioned by the spine and the thighs; at the moment of landing, the strength of the thigh muscles allows a controlled descent through the feet. But in order for the thighs to be effective, the body mass must be centered over the supporting leg or legs and the keystone of the foot or feet. Thus, again, unless the mass of the body is in front of the vertical line of gravity, neither a controlled nor a safe landing can occur.

Newton's Cradles (metal balls of the same size hung on a frame), which grace many desks, can effectively illustrate this concept: When the first ball on one side hits the ball next to it the impulse is carried through the adjoining balls to the last ball, which moves out to the same degree as the original ball. The balls are all aligned and the impulse passes through each center. However, if one of the middle balls is shifted, even slightly, out of alignment, it throws the whole sequence totally out of kilter. In the human structure, the pathway of the impulse affects the jump much in the same way. Any misalignment along the way will compromise the initial push off, will divert the force of that push off, and will render a safe, aligned landing virtually impossible. Additionally, the dancer's body will react to the misalignment by contracting unnecessarily some muscle groups, which will further impact negatively on the performance of the movement and compromise its safety.

Effectively positioning the body mass in front of the line of gravity leads to an awareness of the center of the femoral joint. By maintaining the weight through the center of the joint, we preserve its integrity and avoid sagging or sitting into it. With the pelvis positioned upright, not tilting either forward or backward, the femoral head is free for movement. It is important to remember that turn-out is not a position but a *movement*, the femoral head is rotated within the acetabular cavity and cannot be locked if the legs are to move freely. This, of course, applies equally to the working and supporting legs. Visualizing the action of turning out as a rotating ball (femoral head) when a motion is performed, suggested by Rebecca Dietzel an ideokinesis practionner, is a powerful antidote against gripping in that area.

The awareness of working from the center of the joint is facilitated by the understanding that movement occurs when we move our *bones*. When we have a clear picture of the position to be achieved, we need not concern ourselves with the muscular contractions that will enable us to reach our goal. Our muscles are programmed to move our bones; that is their function. The bones make the shape. As mentioned earlier, in automatic responses such as walking, we do not consciously contract the muscles to move our legs, yet the muscles are engaged. In fact, from the moment we wake up in the morning and sit up in bed our muscles are active and responsive to our wishes. Dance training is a reeducation of our neuromusculature, in other words, we integrate new motions and develop new pathways that eventually become part of our physical vocabulary. This is the principal reason why early training must be based foremost on a concern for good alignment. When the ballet steps practiced in every class are used primarily to instill good habits by testing the ability to preserve alignment while exploring movement possibilities, then the secondary functions of broadening the vocabulary of motion, strengthening, and stretching can be practiced with logic and safety.

Once we move away from the barre to proceed with *adagio* and *allegro* work, alignment acquires another dimension. How we have, with the support of the barre, organized the body weight or mass around the axis becomes of paramount importance. In order to understand this new dimension, two additional terms, the *fulcrum* and *counterbalance*, need to be defined.

In a structure like a seesaw, the fulcrum is the supporting center of a plinth. The plank is balanced when there is equal weight on each side of

Figure 7

the fulcrum. In a human body in motion, the fulcrum is always shifting but nevertheless provides a point of support for each motion. For example, in an *arabesque* the fulcrum is at the top of the supporting leg, the hip joint; the body seesaws forward at an angle corresponding to the height of the extension (see Figure 7).

In a back bend or *cambré* the fulcrum descends down the spine and resides at that point where the vertical and the horizontal lines meet. It initially supports the weight of the head, then more and more of the torso, as the bending becomes more extreme (see Figure 8).

In motions that tilt or take the limbs far away from the axis, the awareness of where the fulcrum is located provides support and facilitates a clear execution.

In one way or another, all motions manage locomotion by *counterbalancing* weight. Motions close to the body's axis require less energy

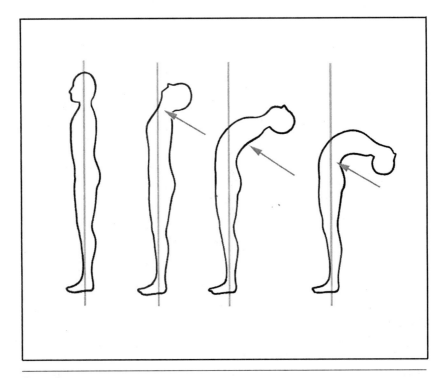

Figure 8

and less muscle power than motions far from the axis; it is easier to lift the leg into a *retiré* (because one's weight is closer to the axis) than to a *seconde en l'air*. Although, inevitably, counterbalancing is present every time a leg is lifted, in ballet it is disguised to a greater or lesser degree depending on the position. For example, in extensions to the back (*arabesque*) the pelvis is allowed to tilt forward, while in extension to the front or side, the body is expected to remain close to the vertical. In both cases, the strength of the inner musculature aids in minimizing the appearance of counterbalance (see Figure 9).

By contrast, some modern styles, like Trisha Brown's, not only reveal but celebrate counterbalance and create thereby a distinctive aesthetic.

Starting from an aligned base in the upright position allows dancers to become aware of the role the center, shifting fulcrum, and counterbalance play in motion. Alignment—the relationship of head, shoulders, pelvis, feet—is the starting point of movement. The concept is addressed in all barre exercises but initially in those exercises that do not involve a high extension, when dancers have an opportunity to concentrate on establishing the relationship of the parts to the whole. This is

Figure 9

why high extensions are not demanded of young, beginning dancers. When alignment is physically understood and the strength to cope with higher extensions is developed, extensions above 90 degrees will test the dancer's alignment; and any adjustments that are necessary can be made by referring back to the earlier exercises.

Alignment is not an end in itself. Like fifth position, it is a tool to be used, manipulated, and adjusted when the body is in motion. But, it is the gateway for all motion; it ensures that the physics and kinetics of dance are in harmony, and thereby predisposes the dancer to work from a secure base that promotes well being.

5

SUCCESSION

Succession refers to motions initiated by the spine that then travel successively through the body:

> Succession is the sequential path of movement through the parts of the body. It operates like a chain reaction, or a wave traveling through the body, moving different parts. As you experience succession in the spine, you will discover how the spine connects the head, shoulders, chest, waist, and how all are connected to the hips (Lewis 1984, 38).

Take the arms as an example: the motion starts from the back lifting the upper arm, activates the elbow, travels down to the wrist, and then to the fingers. This process is reversed with a release of energy. In a way, the impulse is like water flowing through a channel then ebbing back to its origin.

In ballet technique, succession manifests in the linking of details of a specific motion, i.e., the performance of a step, and the connection of several motions into a logical sequence, i.e., *enchaînements*. Moreover, when applied to transitional steps, it helps link the elements of an *enchaînement* into a flowing phrase. Therefore it is relevant to the manner of drawing a leg up into a *retiré,* as well as connecting an *assemblé* to the *glissade* that precedes it, and also to the action of landing and rebounding from a jump. A further distinction can be made if we contrast successive movements, i.e., *développé* with simultaneous movements like *échappé.* Laban defines simultaneous action as "the simultaneous presence of all four Effort elements (Space, Weight, Time and Flow) [that] gives the movement a power of what appears to be self propulsion . . ." (Bartenieff 1980, 63).

A successive motion is like ripples on the water; it engages each part of the body in a logical sequence, in contrast to a simultaneous one that engages all the parts at the same time. To be perhaps overly pedantic, we could say that all motions are successive, but the firing of impulses in jumps or *pirouettes* is so fast that it appears to be simultaneous.

Because this concept addresses how motions unfold, it is important to know where a specific movement originates or where the initial impulse occurs. Movement is initiated proximally but gains in breadth through distal awareness. The ultimate proximal initiation is from the muscles of the spine, but as discussed in Chapter 4, the perception of the involvement of the spine is, in a sense, a negative perception. For example, as we lift a leg to the front, we perceive the movement as occurring in the leg, rather than the activity of the stabilizing deep musculature that we cannot feel to the same degree. A disclaimer is necessary: the following addresses how dancers can facilitate their execution of dance technique through a heightened physical awareness and visualization, and not how movements occur from a purely kinesiological aspect.

The *proximal* initiation is often complemented in motion by the *distal* awareness. In ballet, the spine is held erect and used to support all motions; therefore, it is easier to perceive the hip and shoulder joints as initiators. If the action originates at the hip or shoulder joints, it is proximal; but if the foot or the hand leads the motion, the feeling is distal. This idea should not contradict the earlier claim that all motions originate in the center, because the spine is always engaged in all motions. Distal awareness simply adds another level of expressiveness. The proximal supports and connects to the center, while the distal reaches out and gives breadth to the action, and even force when pushing from the floor. Each is used selectively and often within the same movement.

Taking the arm again as an example: When it moves from a *bras bas* position through 1st to 2nd, the initial motivation is of the humerus in the shoulder joint (proximal initiation). The arm holds its shape. The arm is internally perceived and outwardly seen as moving as a unit. Having arrived in 1st position, the hand begins to lead the motion outward (distal awareness). Of course, the upper arm is also moving, but it is led by the action of the hand. Using the hand to lead the action gives the motion its characteristic generosity; the dancer opens out to the audience and invites them in. In other words, although the arm moves as a unit, the initial impulse (from *bras bas* to 1st) can be felt to occur in the upper arm, then travels in succession through the elbow, the lower arm, through the wrist into the hand and fingers, carrying the energy through to the fingertips, then, as the arm opens to 2nd position, the hand defines the path.

Applying the idea of distal initiation to the legs helps maintain a strong connection to the floor. For example in a *grand battement,* the foot pushing against the floor generates a certain amount of force. A common mistake is to overuse the quads to lift the leg. Although the motion is initiated distally, the hip flexors instantly pick up on the impulse and carry the leg higher. The idea may be best illustrated by the sharing of strength between two dancers. In a simple lift, the female dancer will rise on *pointe* to give added force to her *plié* before pushing off the floor. Her partner will use her upward impetus to lift her higher. The same lift taken from a fifth position without a *plié* and push off is well nigh impossible; because it is very difficult to lift a dead weight. The fact that the floor is an active partner in all motions is recognized through distal initiation.

By contrast, it is useful to think of motions like *développé* as being at the outset proximally initiated; the motion begins in the hip joint, and the thigh, by remaining connected to the deep flexors, can access their strength. The leg becomes light and the dancer can achieve higher extensions. Further, if one thinks of the hamstrings as leading the unfolding, in a way supporting the leg in its upward journey, as the leg stretches the quad will not be overly used. In this case the motion starts with proximal initiation and moves on successively to distal engagement, without loosing the connection in the hip joint, as leg extends. Pushing the leg up from underneath, as opposed to pulling the leg up with the quads, also helps to keep the hip joint free of tension.

With *retirés,* distal and proximal initiations follow each other very rapidly. The initial motion is distal as the foot pushes off the floor. This feature of the motion is important because it conditions the reflex necessary to create torque for *pirouettes.* But no sooner has the push off occurred—the thigh picks up the impulse and the hip joint is activated to lift the leg into place.

Each of the ten barre exercises makes use of either proximal initiation or distal awareness or a combination of the two and, in most, the concept of succession can be experienced. With the first few exercises at the barre, such as *battements tendu, jeté,* or *rond de jambe par terre,* the relation of the hip joint with the pelvis and the foot with the floor are experienced and, in a way, blueprinted for later applications. Initiation of the motion begins with distal awareness of extending the foot into a stretch but instantly involving the hip joint in isolation from the pelvis (see

Chapter 12). Succession is experienced through the smoothness of the actions, out and in for *tendus* and *jetés,* and circular for *rond de jambe.*

The *grand port de bras* at the barre (stretching in deep fourth coupled with *port de bras* and *cambré*), traditionally done at the conclusion of *rond de jambe par terre,* is another example of this concept. As the body bends forward over the front supporting leg, the spine stretches out successively from the sacral area until the impulse reaches the arm that is initially held in 2nd and, as the body stretches forward, moves to 5th. After reaching full stretch, the motion reverses beginning again in the sacral area until it reaches the top of the spine and the body is upright. The arm remains in 5th through the *cambré* back and opens to 2nd as the body returns to the upright position. Both on the forward motion and the return to vertical, the arm moves when the impulse travels through the corresponding part of the spine. The concept of succession can be even more vividly experienced in the *grand port de bras* in the center, when the movement is circular. In this case the body, after reaching the full forward position, circles toward the side then back then returns to vertical (see Figure 10).

Another good example of succession can be illustrated by the *fondu,* where the working leg successively and smoothly unfolds as the supporting leg straightens. After full stretch has been reached, the dancer reverses the action to return to the *retiré* or *cou de pied* position on demi plié. To achieve the quality of "melting," both legs need to stretch and bend at the same rate; the concept of succession can be experienced in this slow unfolding.

The *adagio* vocabulary relies on succession for the lyrical quality that characterizes these motions. When motions are perceived in terms of connections and transitions, with a clear understanding of what each

Figure 10

position requires, the dance phrase acquires a logical flow. One position melts into another, unfolds in a new direction, and transforms as each position, informed by the successive nature of the movement, reaches its limit to begin again. The following *adagio* sequence is one example:

Chassé in an *effacé* direction, to first *arabesque*

The *chassé* provides the initial impulse for the back leg to push off the floor into *arabesque*, the movements are linked by the *plié*.

Shift to *effacé devant* (slow *fouetté en dedans*)

From the *arabesque* the body shifts toward the working leg, which passing through a *seconde en l'air*, ends in *effacé devant*. The action for the *fouetté* is initiated in the hip joint that rotates toward the *seconde en l'air*, bringing the pelvis down to upright (from the *arabesque* tilt) until the leg reaches the front in *effacé devant*. The upper torso follows the pelvis and shifts from the orientation of the *arabesque* to face the opposite direction. In other words, if the *arabesque* is on the right leg facing side # 3 the body will shift to face corner # 8 (see numbering diagram in Glossary.) The motion of the *fouetté* is exactly the same as the Graham spiral exercises, where the pelvis initiates the action and the upper torso follows successively.

Lower the leg through fifth (*coupé*), with the other leg *développé* to *écarté derrière*

As the working leg comes down to fifth position, weight is transferred onto it as the other leg unfolds into the *écarté; développé* begins in fifth the thigh leads the action and the lower leg successively unfolds. Energy is sustained through the change of weight to give the transfer its seamless quality. As with all *développés,* the height of the leg is controlled through the hip joint and placement of the thigh, and the feeling of the motion must be one of lengthening, sending the energy to the toes in order to prevent bunching the quads.

Relevé to half *pointe, tombé dessus,* with the other leg in low *retiré derrière*

In the rise (*relevé*), energy is sent into the floor through the supporting leg to anchor the movement, and ends allowing the working leg to feel heavy, thereby initiating the change of weight by pulling the body naturally into the *tombé.*

Pas de bourrée to fourth position *croisée* (preparation)

The *pas de bourrée* flows out of the *tombé* and transfers weight onto the front leg for the preparation.

Pirouettes en dehors

The *pirouettes* rise out of the preparation, harnessing the force generated by the *plié* and push off.

Finish in fourth *derrière.*

The concept of succession in *adagio* is served by sustaining energy through the transitional moves from one position to another that link the isolated positions and transform the phrase into a danced sequence.

As stated earlier, ballet is ultimately a logical technique; it favors the shortest, most efficient route from one position into another. This factor gives an aesthetic clarity to all motions. In linking steps, the ability to maintain turn-out, and use positions on the floor, such as fifth, as a base to maximize the push off the floor, ensures to a great degree the correct dynamic sequencing of steps. The transitions between one movement and the next will not only be smooth, but will also dynamically engage all the resources of the body to produce the desired effect.

In *allegro* work, succession is closely linked to the actual dynamics of movements. Providing the necessary force to propel off the floor is in fact the function of all preparatory steps; they are designed to facilitate the steps that follow by placing the body in an optimal position to execute the step and by providing a dynamic impulse that will maximize the height of the jump or the torque for *pirouettes*. While in the early stages of training, closing in fifth position between steps is emphasized in order to impress upon the students the clean beginning and ending of each step; in intermediate and advanced work we can focus on the connections. Thus, for example, a *glissade* or *failli* directly serves the push off the floor needed for an *assemblé*, therefore the dancer will pass through the fifth or fourth position, but will not emphasize it. In that context, the preparation is already occurring during the preparatory step allowing the big movement to partake of the impetus created and to be linked through the preparation seamlessly. This can be likened to a singer who carries a phrase on the inhalation of an initial breath. Succession is served when the teacher is fully aware of the dynamics that are inherent in specific steps and—most importantly—has the ability to link steps together without disrupting the flow of energy or conversely to use the flow to create a contrasting move (see Chapter 10).

Succession is also closely associated with weight transference. Certain steps require the body to be carried centrally, while others rely on the weight to be redistributed to favor one side. This is determined by the

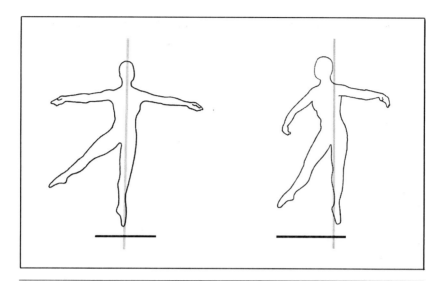

Figure 11

desired height of the jump and the position of the body in the air; if maximum height is required, the impulse from the floor will be vertical, but if the step is a traveling one, then the impulse will adapt to the desired trajectory (Paskevska 1992, 107). My teacher, Cleo Nordi kept a bed-spring in the studio to illustrate this concept. If one pushes with the hand equally on all sides of the spring, the hand is propelled straight upward, but if one favors one side or another, the hand is propelled at an angle. This underlines the fact that *plié* also is a preparatory movement and the pressure through the feet into the floor is a determinant of the direction of the jump. (Male beginners often have a problem with keeping the body vertical during *tours en l'air*. An uneven weight distribution in fifth at the outset of the push off may be a factor.)

As an example of the two types of jumps (one going straight up, the other traveling) we can take *assemblé* and *brisé* (see Figure 11).

Assemblé is a straight up and down jump, so the body is held centrally during the push off and the landing. *Brisé*, on the other hand, travels; therefore the torso shifts toward the direction of travel and the body is carried in front of the line of gravity. The arms also support the forward motion by being placed in 4th *devant* (to the right in *brisé*, the right arm is in 1st and the left in 2nd).

The same considerations are relevant to landing from jumps such as *petits jetés* or *ballonnés* (see Figure 12).

Figure 12

Weight is carried in front of the line of gravity to ensure a safe landing. The same arm as the landing leg is placed in 1st position to emphasize the distribution of weight over the supporting leg (see Chapter 9). However, the positioning of the body in *brisé* is rather more emphatically forward than in the landing of *petit jeté* or *ballonné*, because with the *brisé*, which is both a traveling and a beaten jump, the position facilitates the beat and anticipates the landing. The smooth transition from one step into the next relies both on controlling weight and initiating each step distally to effect the necessary push off that will propel the body off the floor. (Although the subject of dynamics and weight transference will be explored further in the succeeding chapters, these concerns underscore the relatedness between the inner, muscularly initiated proximal impulses, and the outer, distally initiated impulses that rely on contact with the floor and the role of gravity as the inescapable condition for all motion.)

Succession is the connection that links an isolated action to the center from which it can radiate out through the rest of the body. When we are aware of the successive aspects of motion, we can begin to appreciate the logic of the technique. All motions have an inner as well as an outer dynamic component. The inner dynamics rely on the energy created by our body; the muscle power generated by our intention to move. The outer dynamics are conditioned by our relationship to the floor and gravity and include managing our body mass as we propel it through space.

We learn to explore these dynamics initially holding on to the barre, our safety net. Once in the center, managing our body mass without outside support brings a new dimension to the work. A thorough physical understanding of how we generate motion within the body provides an essential insight into managing the body in locomotor activities. Succession is crucial to linking movements internally, as well as connecting steps and phrases. When the initial impulse is successively carried out through the body, the ebb and flow of energy provides fluidity to the transitions. Steps can then be linked into seamless phrases.

6

OPPOSITION

Daniel Lewis explains, "Opposition is a way of using the entire body to create the feeling of length and stretch in a movement, without tensing or gripping ('shortening') the muscles" (1984, 41). The Limón technique defines the six points of opposition as:

    the head
    the left arm
    the right arm
    the left leg
    the right leg
    the spine, in its curling and uncurling process

The feeling of being led by the extremities lengthens and stretches the gesture. Each of the five extremities can oppose the others. For example, the extended arms can be in opposition to the legs, which are reaching into the floor and to the head, which in its stretch is lengthening the spine, while energy through the lower spine is flowing in the opposite direction. Similarly, the arms can be in opposition to each other, stretching in opposite directions, just as the legs can oppose each other, and of course arms and legs can create tension in opposition to the head. The *cambré*, used to illustrate succession, can also complement the concept of opposition. The starting position is a deep fourth, with the back leg extended, the movement forward begins with an oppositional tension between the head and the extended back leg. In the *cambré*, back this opposition continues to lead and travels down the spine until a full arching backward is achieved. In the back bend, the high point is created in the spine as the torso arches. This is the central point through which opposition flows in both directions. In this instance, the use of opposition also complements the idea of fulcrum (see Chapter 4) and gives succession a spatial goal.

The lengthening of the body and limbs has several benefits:

1. Balance is achieved not by muscular contraction, but by opposing forces; the dancer plays with counterbalance and experiences the weight of the limbs in an essentially freeing way.

2. It prevents sitting into the hip joint. The dancer is standing atop the leg, not sinking into the leg. This allows freedom of motion.

3. It adds a dynamic quality to all motions and positions. Although securely grounded through the supporting leg, the dancer looks as if poised for flight.

Steve Paxton (1981–1982, 87) gives us another reason for being awake to the flow of energies within the body, "Contractive energy or tensions overpower the sensing of subtle movement, and so *gravity is masked*" [author's italics]. Working with the concept of opposition encourages a lengthened musculature, allowing the dancer to be aware of subtle changes in gravitational pulls and avoids "muscling" the movement that results in masking gravity.

Awareness of opposition as it manifests in motion, is another way of connecting the whole to the parts. One of its major impacts is on equilibrium. Achieving balance should not be perceived as holding on to a position, but rather as a continuous and imperceptible to the eye adjustment of opposing forces. The concept of opposition enables the dancer to be less concerned with maintaining balance as the oppositional "pull" equalizes the forces acting on the body, lessens the weight of the limbs, and enables the dancer to use the musculature in the lengthened manner that prevents gripping. The head is always reaching upward, the arms and legs are lengthened—transmitting energy from the center. For example, in first *arabesque* the lengthening of the front arm as it reaches forward is balanced by the second arm reaching back, and is in opposition to the lifted leg stretching backward and the standing leg sending its energy deep into the floor, while the head reaches for the sky (see Figure 13).

Contralateral movement is a feature of the human ontogenetic development (Bainbridge Cohen 1993, 5). Infants, in the act of crawling, establish the contralateral pathways that will allow them to move with

Figure 13

efficiency in later life. Carlo Blasis based his discussion on opposition in his well-known 1831 treatise, *The Code of Terpsichore*, on this innate locomotor element, "The opposition of one part of a moving solid to another part is a law of equilibrium by which the gravitating powers are divided. . . . The opposition gives the dancer a very graceful appearance, as he thereby avoids that uniformity of lines in his person so unbecoming a true favorite of Terpsichore" (68).

The concept of opposition, in the classical tradition, manifests most readily through the use of *épaulement*. The torso is placed to create contrast with the front leg: right leg forward, left side of the body forward. It is based on the natural oppositional use of the body when walking, i.e., when the right leg steps forward, the left arm swings forward.

There are two major schools of thought about the use of *épaulement*. The Cecchetti (Beaumont and Idzikowski, 1922/1971, 30) method teaches *épaulement* as a shift of direction; for example in *croisé devant* (right leg front) the whole body turns to corner # 8 (Russian numbering;

Figure 14

Cecchetti numbers the corners and sides separately in an anticlockwise manner, see Glossary). The left arm is lifted to 5th, the right arm is in 2nd position (4th *en haut*), and the head is turned to side # 1. Similarly in *effacé*, the body turns to corner # 2, with arms as above and head turns to side # 1 (see Figure 14, a, b).

By contrast, the Legat System teaches to execute these positions by spiraling the torso; the supporting leg shifts minimally if at all, and the body rotates around its axis. In this system, the positions are initiated by the spine spiraling around its axis in response to the direction of the working leg (see Figure 15, a, b).

By adding the modern dance idea of opposition to Legat's *épaulement*, we introduce another dimension to the performance of these positions; the positions are no longer static but acquire an inner dynamic. For example, in an *effacé devant* position, the right leg extends forward, the left arm lifted in 5th position reaches upward in opposition, the head, turned toward the front, is slightly inclined, in opposition to the left arm as well as the right leg. The right arm extends to 2nd in opposition to the left arm and to the left leg, which is reaching down into the floor. The connection with the spine is emphasized by the upper body spiral, which moves the torso in opposition to the pelvis.

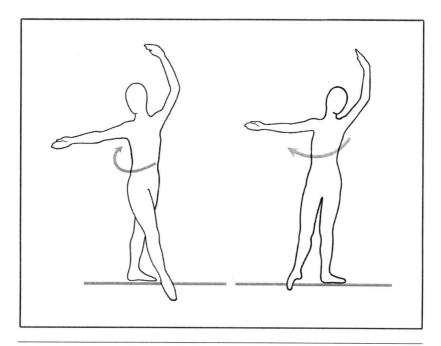

Figure 15

It can be said that opposition is inherently part of ballet training, just as it is part of human ontogeny, "Human development patterns are about integrating the whole body. Built on the reflexes, they begin by connecting head to tail; then they integrate the upper body, the lower body; then all the parts on the same side of the body (eye, arm, torso, leg); the opposite side; and finally the whole body by cross patterns through the center, in what is known as contralateral movement" (Olsen 1991,135). As soon as we open a leg there is a corresponding opposition that occurs on the other side. Thus a *tendu* to the side evokes in the body specific tensions: the working leg is reaching outward, the supporting leg is reaching into the floor. The pelvis on the supporting side is opening in the opposite direction to the working leg, ensuring that both turn-out and stability will be maintained. The energy through the upper torso is reaching upward through the head, while the sacrum is lengthening downward. The arms held in 2nd position are reaching in opposite directions. These oppositional dynamics apply equally whether the leg is lifted off the floor in a high extension or whether the pose is to the front or back (see Figure 16).

Sadly, the dynamic uses of opposition are bypassed when students are told to "pull up" and "hold." These directives also preclude extending the

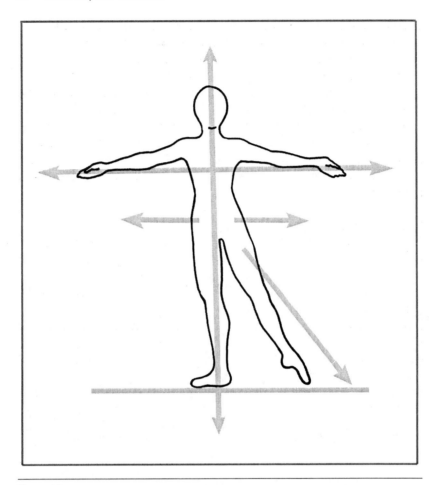

Figure 16

concept to the limbs or, for that matter, to the spiraling motion particular to the execution of *épaulement* (Paskevska 1981, 73). Pulling up has
the effect of disconnecting the pelvis from the upper torso, and thereby
the body from the limbs. As mentioned in Chapter 3, students usually
respond to this demand by sucking in their belly, uplifting their ribcage,
creating a detrimental curvature in the thoracic spine, and, in the process, constricting the diaphragm. Moreover, this positioning impacts quite
negatively on the ability to move with freedom and grace. It impinges
breathing, and disconnects the upper torso from the pelvic area; further,
it hyperextends the psoas muscle by rendering it ineffective in its function of flexion. To lift a leg from this position requires an enormous
amount of muscle power that, of course, results in misalignment and,

ultimately, in overdeveloped thighs. Finally, "hold" conjures up a negative response of overly contracting the musculature and, as Paxton points out, masking the ability to perceive subtle changes.

Urging students to perceive oppositional tensions instead of exhorting them to stretch, also helps to understand the positions within the context of the classical line. Thus, while we may stretch the legs by straightening the knees, we do not stretch the arms by straightening the elbows. In both cases the feeling of extending our reach is internal; with the legs it happens to include the knees, but with the arms it does not include the elbows, which remain always slightly flexed (see Chapter 3, Figure 2).

It must be noted that these concepts are seldom experienced in isolation. Rather, they operate in relationship of one movement to another and often within the same movement, creating a rich palette of sensations to be explored. Let's take a *temps liés* exercise to illustrate their connectedness: From a fifth position, the front foot begins to extend forward, (*croisé devant*) with a distal initiation that in succession draws the leg to full extension. The transference of weight onto the front leg is accompanied by an oppositional extension of the back leg (*pointe tendue derrière croisée*) with, again, distal initiation as the back foot pushes the weight onto the front foot. At the same time, the arms passing through 1st position successively open to 2nd and 5th (4th *en haut*). The motion of the legs and arms sets up an oppositional sequence following the rules of *épaulement* informed by the modern dance concept of opposition; the left side of the body is in opposition to the front leg, the left arm reaching upward in opposition to the right arm extended to the side, both in opposition to the head. At the completion of the motion, the right leg sends its energy into the floor in opposition to the left arm, while the left leg extends back in opposition to the head.

The application of this concept embodies most closely the look of classical ballet. The spiraling of the torso accompanied by the positions of the head creates an aesthetic shape that is unique to the technique and is the best indicator of whether the practitioner really knows the form. It is also the area where the physical and aesthetic are most obviously integrated. The placement of the head in response to the position of the legs ensures that balance will be maintained in the most efficient and, within the aesthetics, the most pleasing way. The ideal "line" is achieved when the legs, torso, and arms form a harmonious picture by an oppositional distribution of tensions. The line of the leg ends in a pointed foot that extends its length, the arms are gently rounded but appear to reach beyond their physical boundaries, the head is poised atop a long neck, the upper back extends or arches as the positions demand.[Opposition calls forth an ebb and flow of energy that trans-lates into kinetic energy.]

The classical technique was developed from the idea of presenting the body at its most harmonious, thus, the line is never sacrificed to expediency, but rather must be achieved within the precepts of correctness. For example, maybe the leg in a *devant en l'air* position could go higher if we tilt the pelvis and ignore turn-out, but this displacement does not serve the line nor our physical well being. Turn-out and height must be achieved honestly. The "look," which is the result of technical and aesthetic correctness, is most in evidence when this concept is honored.

The concept of opposition applied to ballet positions and motions enables dancers to lengthen the breadth of line, helps to maintain the connection between the torso or center and the limbs, and energizes the body. The concept also dovetails the use of *épaulement.* The application of this concept engenders full expressiveness within the vocabulary and ultimately can be used to communicate meaning and emotion.

7

POTENTIAL AND KINETIC ENERGY

The modern dance concept of potential and kinetic energy is very close to the scientific definition of these terms: a ball thrown into the air will gain kinetic energy as it falls:

> Energy is the capacity of the body to move, and *potential* energy is that capacity in its unreleased state, that is, the body on the threshold of movement. *Kinetic* energy is potential energy in motion. In the context of this technique, by potential energy we mean energy that is stored in the body and can be released through gravity. . . . The simplest example of this transformation of energy is a fall (Lewis 1984, 43).

Thus, in the Limón technique *kinetic energy* is manifest when the body falls. *Potential energy*—the body gathering energy prior to the fall—is released by acknowledging gravity. Further, potential energy is trans formed into kinetic energy when the weight of the body creates momentum that causes the body to fall. Less dramatically, the release can be isolated to a particular part of the body, the torso, head, or arm, or even an uplifted leg. For example, when an uplifted arm falls, it re-leases kinetic energy that can be harnessed to create the next movement. In this context it is very much akin to the concept of Doris Humphrey's Fall and Recovery. Release technique specifically, has based its aesthetic on how to become aware of potential energy in different parts of the body and release it into kinetic energy, and then through the momentum redirect the motion. In applying this concept to ballet I'm taking the liberty of interpreting it to include overt action, i.e., storing energy in a run and releasing it in the leap that follows. In this respect the floor is, as always, an active partner of any motion because, in this technique, it is primarily through contact with the floor that we direct, redirect, and propel our body through space.

The body seemingly at rest is vibrant with stored energy that will manifest itself in directed motion when the potential energy is released and becomes kinetic energy. I like to think of the body poised for action as the "engaged body." Thus, even before motion begins there is a feeling of expectancy, an anticipation of all the possibilities that can be explored. The "look" of an engaged body is very different from the look of a relaxed or its opposite, a stressed body. The engaged body is at ease yet energized, conversely the relaxed body does not promise motion, while the stressed body is bound by muscular contractions which in effect prevent motion. An aligned body can be engaged whereas any kind of misalignment will affect freedom by calling outer muscles to the rescue in an effort to maintain equilibrium, and therefore results in a stressed execution. As discussed in Chapter 6, over-contraction of the outer muscles makes us unaware of our inner muscular strength, and further, "If the coordination of their total muscular responses are not balanced so that weight transference through the body falls along the axis of the bones, shearing forces will occur in key areas of joints" (Bainbridge Cohen 1993, 18). In this respect, alignment and intent continue to be of paramount importance; alignment, because the motion will occur from a good base, and intent in its capacity to shape the gesture and direct it on an appropriate pathway.

Bainbridge Cohen further explains muscle contractions that are most relevant to dancers, "A concentric contraction is the gradual *shortening* of a muscle against a resistance. An eccentric contraction is the gradual *lengthening* of a muscle in the direction of an outside force such as gravity, momentum or other muscles" (1993, 19; author's italics). The harmonious give and take between the various muscles groups occurs automatically in an aligned body and, in trusting that process, the dancer avoids dancing by ultimate will power, that is, forcefully contracting the musculature without regard for the actual force needed to perform the movement.

Because of its specific aesthetic, ballet demands a heightened engagement of the musculature before any motion occurs. It is more like the body preparing for flight or fight, rather than a walk through friendly streets. Unlike the aesthetic of post-modern dance that allows a dancer on stage to walk "naturally," in ballet even the walk is specific and energized, at least in the classical repertoire.[1] But, as remarked earlier, we most readily learn by contrast, thus it is through engaging the body that conscious release can be experienced.

Developing awareness and engaging in intentional motions is part of the training of dance disciplines. A technical base demands that one become aware of the gesture. First, of the purely physical sensation, i.e., a bent leg feels different from a straight leg. Then the dancer explores more subtle qualities, i.e., the percussive thrust of *battement frappé* is contrasted with the melting unfolding of *battement fondu*. Each exercise at the barre demands awareness of intent, and each motion's specific quality can be refined beyond rote execution. Ironically, it is the students who have started dance at a very early age that are most resistant to discovering the subtleties of movements. The mechanics of the vocabulary have become automatic and reexamining the inured habits demands a great deal of attention, because these habits have to be brought to consciousness before they can be altered. The task of bringing these sensations to consciousness begins at the barre, because the barre exercises form the building blocks for the combinations in the center. Integrating the dynamics of each exercise provides a varied palette of nuances that are further explored through the *adagio* and *allegro* sections of class.

Energy is stored to be released with intent, whether in a controlled flow like *battement tendu* or a more forceful motion like *battement frappé*. Kinetic energy can also be released *upward*. This may seem to be a contradiction of the basic concept, however the release of potential energy into the floor prior to the movement acts as a *fall* and conditions the quality of the kinetic energy inherent in the movement. In a *grand battement*, for example, kinetic energy is released on the way up (beginning by pushing into the floor to energize the leg) but the weight of the leg brings it down (fall). Less effort is needed on the way down. Descent is not controlled by gripping the quads in an effort to resist gravity, but by a feeling of lengthening the musculature and letting gravity do its work.

After the dynamics of individual exercises are assimilated, coupling exercises can enhance the quality between two contrasting exercises. For example, *battement tendu* and *jeté* can be paired; the first a steady lengthening into full extension and a calm return to fifth, and the second a forceful thrust outward and a lengthened return. *Battement frappé* can be partnered with *battement fondu* or *rond de jambe en l'air*. The percussive extension of the *frappé* is contrasted with the slow melting of the *fondu* or the controlled circling of the *rond de jambe*. A controlled *développé* coupled with a *grand battement* also illustrates how potential energy is stored through a movement (*développé*) and explodes in the *grand battement*. In this case, it is the leg "falling" from the height of the *developpé* that creates the kinetic energy for the *grand battement*.

In slow adagio work, the concept of potential and kinetic energy is very close in spirit to the Limón technique, and can be applied to falls from high extensions (as in *développé* to an *écarté* or *effacé* position followed by a *tombé* and *pas de bourrée)*. Potential energy, vibrant in the *développé*, releases into kinetic energy with the *tombé*, and is gathered again in the *pas de bourrée* to be released in the next movement, for example, a *pirouette*. In this context the concept of succession is also vital, helping to link the succeeding steps.

The concept of potential and kinetic energy can be as easily extended to include jumps. We harness potential energy and transform it into kinetic energy as we propel ourselves into the air. In ballet we refer to this quality as "attack." The actual attack begins with the preparation; the potential energy waiting for release until the push off the floor will launch the jump. The quality of the preparation conditions both the quality and the height of the jump. Therefore, there are different preparations that are used with specific jumps. For example, a *small assemblé* does not need a lot of energy to get off the floor, and a little *glissade* is sufficient to provide a springboard. However, if the *assemblé* needs to be bigger/higher, *tombé* and *pas de bourrée* provide the added momentum necessary to maximize the push off. In an *assemblé volé* preceded by a *failli*, a wide fourth position at the end of the *failli* will furnish the necessary momentum by providing a platform from which to spring commensurate with the intended height of the jump that follows (see Chapter 8).

The bigger the jump, the more momentum needed. For any jump that needs to get as high as possible, a running preparation (a variety of *pas de bourrée couru*) is used. Leaps like *grand jeté, grand jeté en tournant,* and *saut de basque en tournant,* are generally preceded either by a *pas de bourrée couru* or a *chassé*. During the preparation, kinetic energy is held in check; it can be compared to revving the car before releasing the clutch. The power is stored for the moment when the body needs to be propelled upward; but it is already churning, manifested in the undisguised, yet kept in check, energy of the run. Some male dancers like Nureyev, Baryshnikoff, and Bujones, to cite a few of the best, have perfected preparations that are almost as exciting as their jump. The feline quality of the run is its distinguishing feature; the dancers are like panthers chasing a prey, muscles coiled in anticipation of the release into a long high jump. In this context, I remember being totally enthralled by the Limón Company in London in 1956. Although I recall vividly the dances presented, one of the features that impressed me most at the time was Jose Limón coming on stage for his bow. His walk was charged with vibrant energy, it was like a promise, a caress, a tantalizing secret that might never be revealed.

The classical vocabulary does not inherently have "meaning;" it is the interpretive abilities of dancers that transform a position into a feeling state capable of being communicated. But it starts with kinetic energy, controlled, redirected, strongly rhythmic, or lyrical. Once again, the aesthetic qualities have their origin in the physicality of movements. In choreography, the interpretative and expressive qualities of the gesture become a primary concern: What does it mean? How can the intent be conveyed? An *arabesque* is first a lovely line. But it can also express joy, longing, assertiveness, or dismay; and has been used in a variety of contexts by all choreographers. Of course, as soon as we start to move we are releasing kinetic energy, but it is through awareness that control is gained and meaning conveyed.

The concept of potential and kinetic energy is elusive, yet like other concepts that are not expressed in a definite set of actions, pervades the execution of all motions. Dancers capable of consciously harnessing the energy generated by the body and who use the floor effectively are truly in control of the effort required by any set of motions, and, as a result, handle the body with efficiency and beauty.

The unhampered release of potential energy into kinetic energy is best served by an aligned body, clear intent, and precise execution of all motions. The body in motion gathers potential energy through the transitional steps and releases it into kinetic energy as the dancer leaps into the air or twirls in a *pirouette*. Within the sequence, the form is preserved: turn-out is maintained, the shape of the arms enhances the movement, the feet point appropriately, positions are clean, and transitions are accurate. Observing these factors ensures that the aesthetic is apparent: the dancer moves with intent, either with overt force or seemingly without effort. Potential and kinetic energy is communicated through an inner rhythm of contraction and release of tensions like a painter using chiaroscuro to give depth to his image.

8

FALL

In the Limón technique, a fall is another example of the conversion of potential energy into kinetic energy. A fall is a complete release of the muscles as the body, giving in to gravity, drops (Lewis 1984, 43). In this technique, any part of the body can fall. For example, the head may fall but the shoulders remain upright, or the upper torso may fall without affecting the pelvis. There is always a part of the body that acts as supporter or stabilizer, except selectively with falls that end in full contact with the floor. Therefore, within the concept there is the implication of a supportive fulcrum that allows for the free fall of a part.

Modern dance has a rich vocabulary of falls to the floor that is enhanced by a tradition of not hiding effort or disguising the weight of the body. By contrast, in ballet the fall is always somewhat controlled and does not appear to be a surrender to gravity. But in defying gravity, classical dancers need to be aware not only of the object being defied, but also the manner in which it is defied. We can only successfully disguise that which is known. Awareness of the weight of the body and the pull of gravity is a necessary stage in the effort required to perform motions, that is, recognizing weight as an integral part of fall leads to efficiency in motions, because weight can be used as ballast.

Because so much of the ballet dancers' training is focused on control, fall is difficult to appreciate. Moreover, fall in ballet does not have the same "look" as it does in modern dance. Nevertheless, the concept is relevant in terms of weight management and transference, and again highlights the benefits of using the floor as an active partner. Too often ballet training stops short of developing that quality of letting go of overt control. When the path or pattern of a motion is trusted, the execution

[handwritten margin note: awareness of the manner in which gravity is defied]

69

[handwritten note: fall is difficult to appreciate because control]

[handwritten: fall allows movements to appear free, flowing, and dynamic]

of movements appears free, flowing, and dynamic, almost feline; by contrast, when that quality is missing the performance becomes rather tentative and stilted. Margot Fonteyn discovered that quality of letting go when she began dancing with Nureyev. Her interpretations gained a new freedom, almost an abandonment, which seemed to carry her effortlessly and imbued her dancing with a richness and depth hitherto only implied. Additionally, ballet can only seem to defy gravity when the dancer is in total harmony with the laws of physics and with internal/skeletal alignments.

The idea of fall is so closely associated with recovery and rebound, that it is difficult to avoid mentioning them within the present context; therefore the discussion below will include these concepts as they apply to specific movements.

The most obvious example of the fall in ballet is *tombé*, *[handwritten: Class]* which literally means to fall. *Tombé* is a connecting step designed to provide the energy/push for the motion that follows. When the weight of the body is allowed to descend through the leg and foot into the floor, the action of pushing off is maximized. This placement of weight allows for full contact with the floor that gives power to the leg to push off. Similarly, the concept can be extended to *pliés* when they are used as springboards to launch into a jump. This is one of the functions of the fall: to provide, through contact with the floor, a stable pressure to generate the force necessary to propel the leg or the entire body upward or in another direction. Therefore, the concepts of weight prior to the fall, and of recovery and rebound after the fall are integrally part of ballet motions.

A *tombé* can be preceded by either an uplifted leg or a small *sauté (temps levé)*, that is, *tombé* is a motion from up to down ending in a *plié*. (This feature distinguishes it from a *piqué* which is a motion from down to up, i.e., from a *plié* onto a straight leg on *demi* or full *pointe*.) When beginning from an extension, the extended leg can be quite low, 45 degrees off the floor, or in full extension to 90 degrees or higher. From those positions the dancer allows the leg to become heavy and lets the weight of the uplifted leg take her in a free fall to the next position. For example, from a *devant en l'air* position, the uplifted leg drops to a *plié* ending with the other leg extended in an *arabesque* (see Figure 17).

The acknowledged weight of the uplifted leg initiates the action the body follows until the weight has transferred onto the new supporting leg. The other leg is in an extension either off or on the floor.

When a *tombé* is the prelude to pushing off into a high jump (i.e., *assemblé volé,* or *fouetté sauté*),[1] we need to address the degree of displacement that occurs when the working leg is subsequently lifted as the

Figure 17

body is propelled upward. In the words of Rudolf Laban, "The law of counterbalance (tension) demands that any limb moving in one direction be given a counterweight which would be led in approximately the opposite direction, in certain definite measures and angles . . ." (Bartenieff 1980, 101). The body must be placed in an optimum position to facilitate both the push off and the position in the air. Pushing-off is most effective when enough body weight is securely over the leg that is going to be executing the push-off. However, we also have to account for the displacement that will occur when a high extension follows. Therefore the distance between the two legs (in fourth position) must be commensurate with the desired angle of the leg extending *en l'air* to allow for the counterweight to be effective.

For example, in a *assemblé volé* preceded by a *failli (temps levé tombé)*, the leg thrusting upward in the *assemblé* (gesture leg) will push the body in the opposite direction. Ideally, the body is vertical at the height of the jump; the working leg positioned at ninety degrees. Therefore, the position of the body at the conclusion of the *tombé* should be held forward enough of the line of gravity to allow enough space for the body to move to vertical during the *assemblé* (the higher the leg in the extension, the more displacement can be anticipated). In other words, the width of the initial fourth position preparation (the ending position in the *tombé*) with the body weight over the front leg, provides the counterweight for the working leg as it extends to ninety degrees (see Figure 18).

Figure 18

If the fourth position is too narrow, the thrust of the leg will push the body in the opposite direction and will result in a positioning in the air beyond the desired vertical (see Figure 19).

Thus, the width of the fourth position is in direct relationship to the desired height of the leg in extension. That is, if the *assemblé* is at forty-five degrees, the fourth position can be quite small because the body's displacement will be minimal. But if the leg is to be lifted to ninety degrees in the extension, then the fourth position needs to be wider to allow for the shift in the body to vertical.

The mechanics of the *fouetté sauté* are much the same as the *assemblé volé*. The *failli* (*temps levé tombé*) preceding the *fouetté sauté,* places the body forward over the front supporting leg, in order to allow for the displacement that will occur as the back leg thrusts into a ninety degree extension to the front. The same considerations apply to *saut de basque en tournant.* The movement is usually preceded by a *chassé,* a preparatory motion that has the same function as the *tombé* or *failli.* Thus, it is during the *chassé* that the body is held slightly in front of the line of gravity. With the *grand battement devant,* the body returns to center, and the other leg assumes its position in *retiré.* It must be emphasized that placing the body in front of the line of gravity does not mean, in this case, that the torso is leaning forward; rather it is an inner realignment of weight.

Figure 19

Another example of this concept is the execution of *renversé* preceded by *tombé* (see Figure 20). At the beginning of the movement, the body is positioned forward over the front leg (unlike the preceding example, the torso in this movement actually leans over the front leg), recovers to the vertical during the *relevé* and *grand rond de jambe*, and ends forward with a highly arched back at the conclusion of the *rond*, the body returning to vertical with the final *pas de bourrée en tournant*. A wide fourth position, with the body centered over the front leg, allows enough space for the body to shift to a verticality centered over the supporting leg following the push off the floor (*coupé*). Again, when the fourth is not wide enough, or when the body is held too upright, the thrust of the leg upward will cause the body to shift beyond the vertical, and behind the center of the supporting leg. Additionally, placing the weight of the body over the front leg during the preparation allows the dancer to take full advantage of the fall; the pressure on the floor can then provide the strength for the rebound (*grand rond de jambe*). This is the same kind of action as in *grand battement*, described earlier, where the pressure into the floor minimizes the muscular contraction needed to lift the leg up.

Tombé is often followed by a *coupé*. The motion of the *coupé* is downward usually from a low *retiré* position. In this strong downward path,

Figure 20

the leg performing the *coupé* is literally cutting the other leg loose, whether into a *dégagé,* the circular path of a *renversé,* or into a *piqué.* It can also propel the body into a jump as in *coupé jeté.* The *coupé* always cuts close to the other leg, because its function is to find a base at exactly the same place as previously occupied by the other leg. Therefore, using the above example, when the *tombé* ends in a wide fourth position, the *coupé* leg comes under the existing placement of the body, i.e., the back leg performing the *coupé* will be drawn into a low *retiré* immediately behind the front leg while the body maintains the forward lean. The weight shift at that moment is minuscule. The timing of these actions is very fast and details are hard to see. However, if a student has difficulty in finding the standing leg in the *rond de jambe* (*renversé*) or has trouble lifting the leg to ninety degrees in *assemblé volé,* more often than not the cause is in the positioning of the body during the preparation. And, finally, the body angled forward, followed by the recovery to vertical, has a dramatic quality that is completely absent when the movement is performed from upright to upright.

    Coupé-chassé or *temps levé chassé* (Figure 21) is another example of the action of fall. In this movement, the *coupé* can almost be mistaken for a *sauté* because it does not begin in *retiré,* but it does perform its function of freeing the other leg. Thus, the *temps levé coupé* is followed by a fall (*chassé*) onto the front leg. Although the back leg, the one executing the *coupé,* is also the landing leg, the weight of the body is immediately transferred to the front leg (*chassé*), and the sequence is repeated (there is also an *en tournant* version of this movement). During the landing, the two legs are held close together to ensure that the next *chassé* starts from fifth. Considering the *chassé* as a fall, with its concomitant weight transfer, helps to avoid a common problem in the

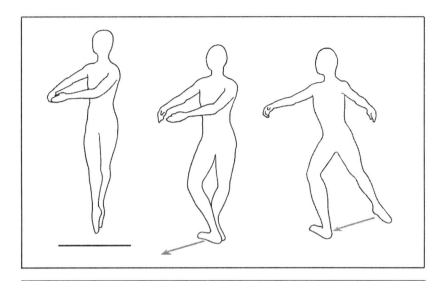

Figure 21

execution of this step, i.e., carrying the body on the back leg, which precludes a correct landing and usually results in a premature opening of the front leg that, in turn, compromises the ability to transfer the body's weight onto that leg.[2] That is, although the back leg is first in making contact with the floor, the weight of the body already favors the front leg, anticipating the full weight transfer onto it.

So far, only *tombé en avant* has been described, the movement coming forward with the body weight transferring onto the front leg. However, there are a few instances when a *tombé* or a *failli* are executed *en arrière*. In those cases, the weight of the body does not transfer completely onto the back leg. Ballet technique takes fully into account the fact that the body is more stable when held in front of the line of gravity, thus when the legs are in a wide fourth position, the weight of the body is carried over the front leg even when the step is traveling backward. *Temps levé chassé en arrière,* similarly to *failli,* retains the body weight over the front leg, thus the mechanics of the movement are slightly different from *en avant;* the back leg extends backward, but the weight remains in front of the line of gravity. This ensures that equilibrium is preserved.

Finally, in extending the meaning of fall to *pliés* as a prelude to pushing off into the air, we acknowledge the dynamic quality of the *plié*. This allows us to use the weight of the body as a vigorous, propulsive force.

In addition to providing the essential physical contact with the floor, fall can also be seen aesthetically as adding modulation to the dance. It is hard to keep one's attention focused when a speaker never changes the timbre or rhythm of his speech. Movement occurs on essentially three levels: with the body on the floor, upright, and in the air. Fall directs the energy below the floor; the dancer digs down into the earth in order to get the strength to ascend to the sky. Thereby, jumps seem to be higher, *pirouettes* more exciting, and positions more emphatic.

The very antithesis of fall was cultivated in the Romantic Era. Charles Didelot is reputed to be the first, in his ballet *Zephyr et Flore*, to make use of wires to create an effect of ethereality. The dancer skimmed the surface of the stage seemingly supported by her toes: "The effect of defying gravity was so desirable that females began to imitate the feat, using their own foot strength" (Lee 1999, 141). Padded shoes were the next innovation in the evolution of *pointe* work, allowing the dancer to create the illusion of ethereality without the restrictive use of wires. The ballet slipper evolved and was commercially available by the 1880s, providing more support to the instep and more protection to the toes. The ability to dance on *pointe* became the hallmark of the classical dancer (Barringer 1990). In this evolution, the quality of earthiness achieved by emphasizing the role of the torso in weight transference, which is also part of the ballet aesthetic, was somewhat obscured. Similarly, the super uprightness favored by some ballet styles can have the impact of minimizing the connection with the floor; the resulting execution of motions is rather brittle and somehow unfinished or unfulfilled. Gravitas can be recaptured when the concept of fall is fully manifest.

In using the concept of fall in ballet, we take into consideration the shape or aesthetics of ballet movements; there is no equivalent in this vocabulary of the abandonment experienced in modern dance. However, fall also addresses the awareness of the weight of the limbs on their downward trajectory (as in *tombé* from a high extension), weight transference in its function of facilitating locomotor movement, and efficiency in the use of the floor when the weight of the body encourages full contact prior to pushing off. In this respect, the concept is central to the understanding of ballet technique.

9

WEIGHT

Daniel Lewis's description of the the use of weight in the Limón technique is equally applicable to ballet:

> The use of weight is the hardest element of Limón technique to define and apply because it is itself a quality of movement. Within a technical aspect of a movement, such as opposition or suspension, weight is added by isolating a part of the body and allowing it to succumb to gravity while maintaining the suspensions, oppositions and high points in the rest of the body (Lewis 1984, 44)

As Lewis states, weight is a quality of motion; it is a physical sensation that gives rise to an aesthetic manifestation. In Chapter 8, we explored the use of weight in the context of fall. Now, we will explore both the qualities that weight adds to the execution of the vocabulary and its use as a ballast to facilitate motions. "Isolating a part of the body and allowing it to succumb to gravity" while maintaining the shape and energy in other parts of the body is another aspect of motion that is at the very core of ballet training.

In one way or another, all of the previous concepts that we explored have a bearing on weight. Working from an aligned base ensures that the appropriate muscles are called into action, which affects the way we perceive our body in motion, and helps us manage the weight of the limbs. Succession makes us aware of the relationship between the different parts of the body, hence their weight. Opposition encourages an awareness of the connectedness between the various parts of the body and, by redistributing the weight, makes the limbs feel light. Potential and kinetic energy make us aware of the force stored in our body and lead to an appreciation of our relation with the floor and gravity. Finally, fall has everything to do with managing weight.

While much of ballet training is directed at hiding both the weight and the effort, it is also concerned with fostering groundedness, that is, energy flows through the legs and feet into the floor to ensure a stable base. Dancers who are not aware of their weight or the nature of the effort of a motion cannot experience the technique in its fullness, nor can they create the illusion of weightlessness and ease when it is choreographically necessary. Ballet's focus on either disguising or redirecting weight is the opposite of denying; we recognize an object and choose to hide it. However, hiding the effort can be achieved most directly only when the movement occurs from an aligned stance and the origin of that movement is understood. For example, we all know that the distal part of a limb, like the hand or foot, is not what is holding the limb up, yet students commonly attempt to do a *retiré* or a *développé* without engaging the thigh (which also means that the psoas muscle is not activated). To understand that the movement requires the engagement of the thigh, encourages a connection with the psoas, hence the deep musculature. It ensures that the motion in the hip joint is free of tension, and thereby the weight of the leg is disguised. A crane used for raising, lowering, and shifting heavy weights provides a graphic image for this mechanism: the vertical support is connected to the horizontal extension by a right angle "joint" through which pass the cables used to carry the building materials. The weight of the load dangling at the end of the line is borne ultimately by the vertical structure and the strength of the cables running through its core.

Dancers, while striving for lightness and avoiding the appearance of succumbing to gravity, must be aware of and able to manage weight and effort. This awareness begins with appreciating the role of the deep muscles connected to the spine that support all overt action.

In our language, we use the word "weight" to denote importance or deep meaning. Light (weight), on the other hand, often refers to something frivolous. Accentuating the quality of "prettiness" of particular movements tends to distance the dancer from the full visceral experience of the movements, and in effect trivializes the classical technique. In the pursuit of prettiness, the quality of weight is disenfranchised. Conversely, when weight is acknowledged and managed efficiently, the intent of the motion can be fully realized. Not only can character or feeling become evident, but the kinetic qualities of motions can be fully experienced and communicated. The harmonious fusion of light and weight depends to a great extent on the understanding of the impact managed weight can play in the execution of motions and in creating the aesthetic.

Thus, awareness of the weight of our body affects the quality of all movements.

In Chapter 8, we discussed managing weight as a tool in mastering the execution of certain steps; using the concept of fall in *failli* or *tombé* to maximize the push off the floor. In that instance we considered the totality of the body's weight. But modern dance often addresses the concept of weight by isolating a specific body part and allowing it to "succumb to gravity." Considering the subject from that perspective can help focus attention on the weight of arms and legs and explore the effect it bears, not only on the quality of motion but also on efficiency of execution.

Ballet training teaches us to control the legs in such a way as they not only appear light to the viewer, but also are perceived as light by the dancer. To achieve this goal, motions of the legs rely on alignment, that is a redistribution of weight to place the body fully on its support and reliance on the inner musculature of the spine and pelvis. Nevertheless, there are exceptions when allowing the leg to be heavy (acknowledging its weight) is necessary for correct execution. In some of these cases the working leg is used, in a sense, as ballast. These motions include *battements en cloche* and *grand fouetté en tournant*, instances where the weight of the leg is an essential part of performing the movements with ease.

The *battements en cloche* partakes of this quality of recovery, yet including this movement in the discussion of weight is also relevant because it allows us to stress this particular aspect of the motion. *Battements en cloche* usually begin in a preparation to *pointe tendue,* either *derrière* to kick front or *devant* to kick back. The notion for this preparation is the same as that of the football player who draws his leg back before kicking the ball; this gives more power to the kick. After the initial kick, the weight of the leg generates its own power as it swings from front to back, but power is generated only if the leg is allowed to be weighty. The leg acts rather like the pendulum on a grandfather clock, which needs to be weighted at the bottom in order to swing back and forth.

The starting position for *grand fouetté en tournant* is in *arabesque.* A sharp *plié* and *relevé* is followed immediately by a swing of the back leg to a *devant* position on half or full *pointe.* The arms come through 1st position and rise to 5th. If only half a turn is required, the body turns away from the uplifted leg immediately ending in *arabesque* (back to the audience); but if a full turn is executed, the *devant* position is held until the third corner (to the right; the leg is held in front until corner # 6) at which point the body shifts into the *arabesque* (see Figure 22). In other words, as long as the leg is held in front, the body will continue spinning.

Figure 22

As soon as the *fouetté* (turning away from the uplifted leg) occurs, the momentum will be stopped. Thus, in theory, the *grand fouetté en tournant* can conclude facing any direction one chooses. It is the weight of the leg swinging from back to front that provides the impetus for the turn. The leg is caught in the *devant* position, and held there until the desired ending direction is reached, at which point the *fouetté* occurs (the body turns away from the extended leg resulting in a finish in *arabesque.*)

Another version of this *fouetté* starts in a *seconde en l'air* position and swings across to *devant* to end in *attitude* (this movement is usually done on *pointe* and in a series). The positions may be different but the mechanics of the motion are the same. The weight of the leg on the downward journey provides the ballast for the extension to the front. The motion is sustained, "caught," and, as the body turns away from the extended leg, becomes an *attitude.* This manner of performing the *fouetté* underscores the difference between using strength (muscling) and taking advantage of the physics inherent in the movement, and thus executing it using one's technique. I have suggested that the evolution of ballet technique relies on possibilities and potential for motion. Taking this thought further, the movements of the technique are designed to allow us to use our musculature efficiently in partnership with the floor and gravity. Muscling is inefficient because it denies the natural flow of motion and is ultimately coercive (coercion is not a good idea either in life or in dance).

As discussed in Chapter 8, a *tombé* from a high extension uses the weight of the uplifted leg to carry the body to a new position. An *écarté devant* position followed by a *tombé pas de bourrée* can serve as example. From a high extension, the dancer rises on half *pointe* (moment of suspension), then allows the leg to become heavy and to pull the body forward into the *tombé,* with the *pas de bourrée* that follows providing the recovery to verticality. In other words, the *pas de bourrée* acts as a break to the forward impetus generated by the fall. Further, no extra muscular contractions are needed to effect the transition from the verticality of the extension to the forward impetus of the *tombé*; the weight of the leg will fuel this transition.

The weight of the limb can also help in transitions from a high jump when a change of direction is desired. With a *grand jeté en avant,* for example, followed by a *pas de bourrée* in the opposite direction (upstage), the weight of the back leg (in *arabesque* after the landing) leads the body in the transition. The momentum of the leap is carrying the body forward; after the landing, the back leg is in *arabesque* and reaches out (opposition) to redirected the impetus in the opposite direction. The redirection begins while the leg is still uplifted and the feeling of weightiness continues through the *pas de bourrée* as it travels upstage. (Another version of this movement will be discussed in Chapter 10.)

Because the arms are non-weight bearing, it is more difficult to feel their weight. But when an arm is lifted with consciousness of its weight, the movement gains in gravity and import. Just as with legs, but in a subtler way, it is important to recognize in using arms the two opposing forces that act upon them: the weight of gravity pulling them down and the muscular effort that brings or keeps them aloft. It is well to remember that the arm is not lifted by the arm muscles but by the back. The muscles of the arm are only engaged in preserving the shape of the position. The awareness of the opposition of gravity (pulling it down) with muscle power (keeping it aloft) gives *port de bras* meaning; the arms are no longer floating in space, at times assuming pretty positions, but are expressive partners cooperating fully in every motion. The old adage "if you're not for me, you're against me" can be aptly applied to the role arms assume in motion. When they are not used consciously to help motion and maintain equilibrium, they act as distracters and affect deeply and often negatively the way weight is managed. This applies both to jumps and *pirouettes.*

The most common mistake is to lift and hold the arms with the shoulder muscles. This execution disconnects the arms from the back, lifts the scapula, and builds up the deltoids. From this base, it is impossible to perform *port de bras* fluidly or to truly feel the weight of the arm. Conversely, from a totally aligned position, with shoulder girdle open and deltoids smoothed out, the arms can move with freedom from the shoulder joint carried by the muscles of the back. They act as stabilizers in most motions; in *pirouettes* they capitalize on the torque created by the feet then stabilize the turn. With jumps, the arms help bring the body aloft and again stabilize the position in the air. But they can perform these services efficiently only if their movement is initiated from the back and their weight is recognized.

The head is yet another part of the body that hides its weight. It weighs between fourteen and twenty pounds and must to be managed in order to ensure that equilibrium is maintained. The technique addresses this concern by positioning the head either over the front leg or over the supporting side of the body. The rules of *épaulement* are a good example. These rules can be explained from three different points of view:

1. Historically, the eighteenth-century ballerina was intent on pleasing the audience and made sure that her focus remained toward the public.
2. Technically, *épaulement* and its accompanying head positions, follow the precept of opposition expounded first by Pierre Beauchamps (Lee 1999, 76) and later by Carlo Blasis (1831, 67).
3. Physically, the head is too heavy to be carried behind the line of gravity, thus the *épaulement* positions also ensure that equilibrium is maintained; whether in *croisé, efface,* or *écarté,* the head is always placed to enhance and most importantly to facilitate the position or movement.

The first explanation may seem rather frivolous in the post-modern era, when the audience's pleasure is seldom a concern: As Sally Banes states, "The breakdown of the distinction between art and life... the clarification of individual, discrete movements, the isolation of the essential characteristics of dance, have all become valid purposes for making dance. So has the option of making a dance for the pleasure of the dancer, whether or not the spectator finds it pleasing or even accessible" (1977, 16). However, the public's approval and therefore attendance at performances cannot but remain of concern in contemporary ballet choreography, even if the means of pleasing have a different aesthetic.

Much of our communication power comes from the face and specifically the eyes; when we want someone to pay attention to us, we look at them. It is the eyes, looking straight out, that give the dancer the quality of aplomb or self-assurance and complete composure. However, the tenets of ballet have never demanded a slavish frontal focus, but rather favor turning or tilting the head to enhance a position, with the gaze oriented in the same direction as the head.[1]

The second and third explanations are related and testify again to the fact that physicality and aesthetics are inseparable in ballet. All aesthetic precepts are based on physical possibilities. Blasis's rules were founded on sound physical evidence that has held true through the evolution and, sometimes, even metamorphosis of the technique. The head is not only angled toward the audience, but is placed either over the supporting leg (if it is the front leg) or turned toward the front leg (if it is in an extension), which ensures that the weight of the body will not be held on the back leg and thus affect equilibrium negatively. For example, in a *croisé derrière* position, the head is set over the supporting leg and is angled toward the audience, whereas in a *croisé devant* position the angle toward the audience ensures that no weight will be spilled over onto the back (supporting) leg (see Figure 23) Note: the position of the head is the same in *croisé devant* as in *croisé derrière* done with the other leg (right leg in extension front or left leg in extension back.) In *écarté devant* position the head is emphatically lifted up in the direction of the up-lifted arm, in harmony with the slight sideways tilt of the body, while in *écarté derriére* the head is turned toward the arm in 2nd position, the focus angled down. In both positions the tilting head/body counterbalances the uplifted leg.

All positions follow this simple precept: the weight of the body is carried in front of the line of gravity, allowing maximum control of all

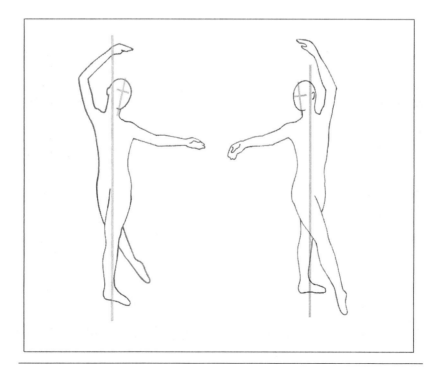

Figure 23

motions. The head is poised centrally in accordance with this alignment. Additionally, the atlantoaxial joint (the connection between the spine and cranium), like all joints, is never locked; this allows the head to be balanced on top of the neck without undue tension, rather like a ball on the tip of the nose of a circus seal.

Although weight is often used very differently in modern dance, the concept of weight is relevant to all techniques inasmuch as it is an inescapable feature of our physicality and therefore affects every aspect of motion. Furthermore, the rules governing the technique, such as head positions in *épaulement*, are designed to facilitate motion and demonstrate the deep wisdom of the technique in the actual practice of the art form.

10

RECOVERY AND REBOUND

Both recovery and rebound happen as a reaction to the release of potential energy; the energy generated by the fall is "rechanneled" into another motion. In the words of Daniel Lewis:

> The end result of recovery and rebound is the same: the potential energy released in a fall is accumulated at the bottom of the fall and rechanneled. In a recovery, the energy passes through the bottom of the fall and continues in the same path, like a swing of a pendulum. . . . In a rebound, it is the elastic reaction of the muscles that is utilized (1984, 44).

Recovery uses the momentum generated by the fall, while rebound characterizes the actual contraction of the musculature to effect a motion. When the fall reaches the lowest point the movement is redirected muscularly. This concept highlights both a physical and a qualitative factor of many steps.

The body in motion is in a constant state of recovery and rebound. How little or how much muscular energy is used is a physical factor; however, how little or how much is allowed to be seen pertains to the area of aesthetics. Nevertheless, whenever we come to a low point, such as *plié* or *tombé*, or when the weight of a limb is used to create momentum, the movement that follows is a recovery or a rebound depending on the degree of muscular contraction necessary to perform the motion.

Laban Movement Analyses gives us yet another way of perceiving the ebb and flow of motion:

Moving in the kinesphere[1] away from the body into even one direction causes a tension between the body and the point reached. Spatial tensions develop in constantly changing degrees throughout the whole path, not just between the beginning and end of it. They are not isolated tensions, but are interdependent with other systems of tensions within other body-space configurations (Bartenieff 1980, 105).

This idea could as easily apply to succession, opposition, or even to fall. In the present context, it underscores the notion that recovery and rebound occur in conjunction with specific shapes and pathways that create degrees of tension.

Grand battement balancé or *en cloche* and *grand fouetté en tournant* are some of the steps in the balletic vocabulary that illustrate recovery. These steps were discussed in Chapter 9, but we will briefly look at them again in this new context. The word *balancé* refers to a playground swing and *en cloche* even more graphically recalls the swinging arc of a bell. In the *grand battement* the leg smoothly kicks and falls to recover by swinging along the same path in the opposite direction, passing with each fall through first position. This brief contact with the floor can also create added impetus for the next kick, rather like a flat stone skimming across the calm water of a lake. However, contracting the muscles of the leg (beyond the contraction already present in a stretched leg) with each swing will only impede the motion. Thus, it is the momentum created by the swing that lifts the leg up, skimming through first position but not stopping there. The weight of the leg in the swing downward powers the leg in its upward path; no additional muscular contractions are needed. The same mechanisms pertains to *grand fouetté en tournant,* but in this instance when the swinging leg reaches the *devant* position it is caught there and held until the rotation of the body places it in *arabesque.* (Inexperienced dancers often attempt to control the swing only to find that the impetus necessary to both lift the leg *devant* and to effect the turn are missing, and they vainly strive to create that impetus with the torso.)

The concept of recovery can also be applied to the action of arms as they swing down, passing through *bras bas,* and continue upward to 5th position. This action is used in *grand fouetté en tournant* as well as in big jumps like *saut de basque* or *grand jeté en tournant.* The momentum created by the fall to *bras bas* not only carries the arms upward but, by engaging the torso and raising the center of gravity, maximizes the force of the push off the floor. In motions like these, we need only let gravity act on our body; there is no effort in fall as there is no effort in recovery if we let our limbs create their own momentum and transfer that power to the torso.

Rebound requires more directed control, and it is easier to recognize within the balletic vocabulary when applied to jumps. The idea of fall and rebound can be applied not only to the landing of all jumps but also to the moment just before the push off into a jump. If we recognize that the *plié* before the jump is the fall, then the next movement becomes, logically, a rebound. For example, with a *glissade* and *assemblé*, the *plié* preceding the jump is the fall; the push off is the rebound. Or to return to our first example, the preparation (*chassé* or *pas de bourrée*) preceding a *saut de basque en tournant*, gathers momentum for the leap; the final *plié* before the push off is the low point that is followed by a muscular push off or rebound. The landing from the jump can also be followed by a rebound or *temps levé* into the next motion. At that point, the body can be redirected onto a new path.

As an example, we can take a short *enchaînement,* traveling downstage: *pas de bourrée couru, grand jeté, temps levé,* followed by a change of direction traveling upstage with *pas de bourrée, grand jeté entrelacé.* During the first two steps the impetus of the body is carrying us forward; the rebound of the *temps levé* breaks the forward momentum and allows us to change direction to execute the last two steps. If the *temps levé* is omitted, the shifting of the momentum is slowed down as the weight of the body regroups to change direction. In all likelihood, unless the dancer uses the weight of the back leg to redirect energy (as described in Chapter 9), he will need to use the torso to shift weight, instead of relying on the rebound that allows a more graceful and more rapid transition. It is quite like changing gears in the car. If one is traveling forward, one cannot simply go backward without stopping and passing through neutral. The *temps levé* acts like on the application of the brakes before shifting and provides the opportunity to reorganize the weight to allow for a change of direction. And, of course, it is one of Newton's laws that a moving object will continue to move in the same direction unless stopped by an outside force; in this case the *temps levé* through contact with the floor provides the outside force.

While recovery relies on the weight of the limbs, rebound often depends on the ability to strongly push off the floor. Both the awareness of the weight and the ability to push off are nurtured in the barre exercises when closing between motions in a clean fifth position with weight on both feet is emphasized. In exercises such as *battements tendus* or *jetés,* among others, there is a subtle transfer of weight each time the leg returns to fifth (from one foot to both), and a strong initial connection to the floor each time the leg opens to *pointe tendu* or to the *en l'air* position. I have witnessed teachers setting a breakneck speed for these exercises, reasoning that it builds the ability to move fast. However, moving fast depends on accuracy of contact with the floor, that is, creating a secure base from which to rebound. When *tendus* and *jetés* are executed too fast, there is no opportunity to experience the precise mechanics of the movements, muscles are in a constant state of over tension, and a transfer of weight cannot occur. And while the dancer may feel challenged by the speed, without the weight transfer the exercise does not prepare for quick *allegro* motions when weight transference is at the very core of the movement.

The aesthetic of recovery and rebound is probably best illustrated by the quality of *ballon* inherent in the allegro vocabulary. As such, it cannot be isolated from the concepts of fall and weight. Recovery and rebound follow fall and rely on the exact management of weight to create the illusion of effortlessness. It is also closely linked to potential and kinetic energy (see Chapter 7). The dancer stores potential energy in a running preparation and lets kinetic energy explode in the leap, then rebounds in another direction, twists and turns, dips down, and reaches up. The concepts of fall, weight, rebound, and recovery complement the concepts of potential and kinetic energy and inform the motions imbuing them with the aesthetic quality of vitality.

Recovery and rebound expresses the idea of *joie de vivre* in motions characteristic of the Bournonville style. A Bournonville jump always includes a rebound after the landing, thus a *grand jeté* is followed immediately by a *temps levé* that de-emphasizes the landing and adds lightness to the phrase. Similarly, *petit allegro* steps follow each from rebound to rebound. This style can be contrasted with that of the choreography typical of the Soviet ballets where after a big jump the landing is held, as for example in the male variations in *Spartacus*.

For some ballet dancers, who have been taught to rely entirely on the strength of their muscles, trusting the path of a movement and allowing the weight of the body to carry a motion does not come easily. It seems to contradict everything they have come to know in terms of effort and control. Vera Kostravitskaya criticized some dancers overreliance on muscular strength:

> At times . . . there appear "innovators" who offer to introduce some elements of acrobatics or their own accelerated method of developing the leg muscles. Most frequently, these are various limbering exercises that lead to professional injuries. Although all of them are claimed to be new methods, in fact, they have been

known for a long time and were formerly used, although, as a rule by bad teachers (1979, 18).

In other words, effort is always commensurate with the intention, both physical and aesthetic of a movement, and equating muscle bulk with strength may apply to weight lifters but not to dancers. We need to expunge the words "working hard," and replace them with "working well"; in doing so, we need to look to the technique to reassess our assumptions as to the effort actually necessary to perform movements. In this task, we become conscious of the inner muscular resources of the body and, it can be said, begin to truly dance from the center.

When the concepts of recovery and rebound coupled with weight and fall are practiced, the body responds with the appropriate muscular contractions. There is no need to coerce the body into motion, only to let the weight of the limbs generate the force needed and to allow the motions to flow. These qualities support the execution of the vocabulary and are already inherent in the technique. We need only to recognize them and to put them to use.

11

SUSPENSION

Like opposition, suspension is a feeling created internally that becomes manifest externally in the quality of the motion, "A suspension is a prolonged high point. It is created at the peak of the movement by continuing the movement and delaying the takeover of gravity" (Lewis 1984, 44). Suspension is like a hesitation between two actions; an in-breath delayed before being let out. The pause causes a heightened anticipation, a tension between the motion that is ending and the motion that follows. This quality allows for space and contrast to be created between forceful actions. It can be experienced in conjunction with opposition in movements that require sustained balance and also as a connection or bridge from one action to another. In ballet, we recognize it in phrasing and even sometimes refer to it as musicality; however, in linking it to musicality, in the present context, we must be careful to preserve its physical aspects.

Balancing in a position is often perceived as having to hold that position. Holding generally results in contractions that shorten muscles. Holding does not provide more stability but rather prevents the body from reacting to the changes occurring internally; it masks our ability to appreciate the subtle inner adjustments that keep us in equilibrium. Gymnasts doing a routine on a beam can show the adaptations necessary to keep their balance; they can shift their torso back and forth and move their arms to preserve balance. These moves even serve to heighten the viewing public's pleasure and appreciation because they can see the difficulty of the task. Ballet dancers must hide these adaptations, but not through denial and contraction. The feeling of opposition that lengthens the musculature and the feeling of suspension that prolongs a motion provide the means of hiding without denying or contracting.

The word "balancing" implies adapting; adding or subtracting weight balances the scales. Keeping energy flowing through the body allows us to both adapt and hide the process. For example, in a fifth position on *pointe* with arms also in 5th, there are several oppositional channels of energy flowing through the body. The first, down from the hip joint to the tips of the toes, keeps the dancer anchored to the floor for stability. The second, up from the pelvis (pubic bone) to the center (twelfth thoracic), ensures that the weight does not sink into the hip joints and relates to the third channel down from the shoulders into the center. The second and third channels engage the torso and maintain the length of the spine, as well as anchor the arms at the shoulder joint, while the fourth flows outward through the fingertips. The fifth channel flows from the sternum upward through the head. The internal experience of this pose, as well as any other held position, is one of constant subtle shifting, adjusting, feeling the ebb and flow of energy coursing through the body (see Figure 24).

The external perception is somewhat of an illusion; the spectator does not see the adaptations only a body miraculously suspended in time and space. The concept of suspension further enlivens the pose and enhances the illusion; the dancer takes a breath, prolongs the pause, and redirects the energy into another motion, possibly a fall and rebound. An example of this sequence can be seen in the Prelude of *Les Sylphides* where a rise to fifth position and a suspension, while the torso moves from right to left, is followed by a *tombé, coupé,* and *assemblé.* The pose in fifth is dynamically connected through the breath to the motion of the torso. The dancer yields to gravity in the *tombé,* and redirects the energy through the *coupé* into the *assemblé.* (Even the *assemblé* in this sequence can be perceived as a suspension if the dancer retards the action of the arms only dropping them down after she sinks into the *plié.*)

These flows and ebbs punctuated by suspension are experienced in an exercise routinely performed in *pointe* classes. Four *ballonnés* (in *effacé*) are performed springing on *pointe.* The first and second are done with a *relevé* with each *ballonné;* the dancer holds the third *relevé* on *pointe* while the working leg executes two more *ballonnés.* As the supporting leg executes the *relevé* for the third *ballonné,* the downstage arm, previously in 1st, rises to 5th position. The upper body is placed slightly behind the line of gravity to counterbalance the weight of the leg extended forward. But it is the arm rising to 5th that (increasing the feeling of opposition) leads the suspension. This lengthening and extending al-

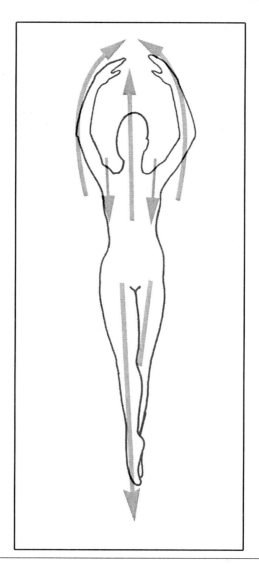

Figure 24

lows the dancer to remain on balance, suspended, on *pointe* while the working leg bends and stretches twice.

As another example we can take the *temps liés* exercise described in Chapter 5. Beginning as we did before in fifth position, right leg in front, extending the front leg to a *croisé pointe tendue*, transferring weight onto the front leg and extending the back leg in *pointe tendue*, as this sequence reaches its peak and the arms are in 4th position (left arm overhead, right arm in 2nd), the motion, in a fully oppositional extension, is suspended for an instant, before the back leg closes in fifth. Then, the other leg extends to *pointe tendue* in *seconde*, supporting leg sinking into *plié*, the suspension sustaining the transition until the overhead arm comes down to 1st position and sweeps to 2nd as the weight transfers to allow the previously supporting leg to extend into *pointe tendue*. The weight then transfers to the previously extended leg, the other leg in *pointe tendue* in *seconde*. The arms are extended in 2nd, and the motion is briefly suspended before the leg closes in fifth and the movement is performed on the other side.

The success of suspension is to a great degree dependent on the feeling of opposition. When a motion has arrived at a position, as for example an *arabesque*, opposition gives it length and line, just as the position is about to change, maybe with a *tombé* that swings the leg through first to a fourth position *devant* (fall). The *arabesque* is suspended for an instant, and seems to extend even further, floating, then dissolves into the next motion. If the *arabesque* in on *pointe,* the effect is heightened because, as with the *ballonné* exercise, the suspension allows the dancer to stay on *pointe* a little longer and to present greater contrast between the held pose and the fall.

It is probably with high jumps that the concept of suspension can be most dramatically experienced. Nijinsky, Nureyev, and Baryshnikov had perfected that moment of suspension in their jumps, when they appeared to be floating in the air. Of course, it is the quality of the jump that creates the impression or illusion of a body hovering in the air, because not even these dancers can resist the pull of gravity.

Several factors make this feat possible:

1. The jump itself must be high enough.
2. The arms are held aloft, to enhance the illusion and distract the spectator, who does not see that the dancer is already in the process of descending—rather like a magician who draws attention to his right hand while the left disposes of the object. In jumps like *grand jeté entrelacé*, the arms remain overhead until the landing, or open to a high *allongé* position at the height of the jump to emphasize the moment.
3. The use of suspension: With a *grand jeté*, for example, at the apex of the jump the dancer increases the split of the legs, which adds height to the jump and seems to delay the moment of descent.
4. The ability to get into a specific position quickly and to maintain it through the descent as in *double saut de basque en tournant*, also aids in the illusion.

Another remarkable aspect of these suspended jumps is the ease of ascent. There is nothing brittle to undermine the feline quality of the preparation and the subsequent leap. The potential energy is held in check, yet it imbues the motion with power that erupts in the release of kinetic energy as the dancer takes to the air. Even before the apex of the jump is reached, the dancer seems to be hovering. Suspension is prolonged because the feeling encompasses the ascent as well as the beginning of the descent.

The aesthetic of suspension is recognized in phrasing/musicality and in balancing (sustaining a specific position.) Phrasing/musicality is not slavishly following a musical phrase, but rather a prolonging or a shortening of the physical action that serves to underscore the flow of the music. Catching the up beat of the musical phrase is characteristic of ballet's creative use of tempi and is most in evidence within the *allegro;* the dancer anticipates the up beat beginning the preparation on the "and," reaching the apex of the jump on "one." By contrast, in *adagio,* motions tend to trail the musical phrase, which results in intensifying the lyrical quality of the movements. Balancing or prolonging a state of equilibrium is often included within that elongation of action. It can also become almost a cliché when the moment of suspension is used to highlight the end of a motion, as in the Rose Adagio when Aurora, after the *promenade* in *attitude,* balances in the pose before taking the hand of the next suitor to repeat the sequence.

Thus both musicality and phrasing rely on suspension, the former in terms of synchronizing the motion with the music and the latter by using the music creatively; that is being with the music but not being tied to the beat. Fokine's choreography in *Les Sylphides* is a good example of this kind of usage: "In *Les Sylphides* there is a unique style. While still, one must be always on the brink of movement" (Makarova 1979, 118). Fokine bridges musical phrases by having the corps de ballet move on the fourth beat of a 4/4 phrase instead of keeping the dance sequence squared to the music by moving on the first count of the next phrase. The dancers are seen as if floating atop the music. In the Mazurka variation, the dancer executes several *pirouettes* in *arabesque.* With each pirouette she springs on *pointe* on the first count of the bar, again creating the quality of suspension. In fact, all *pirouettes* share the quality of suspension. While firmly grounded to the floor through the supporting leg, the dancer hovers in the spin. Baryshnikov is among the first male dancers to have perfected the ending of *pirouettes* as a sustained motion. Instead of finishing with both feet on the floor, he winds down to a stop while remaining on half *pointe.* There seems to be something miraculous in this ability to control impetus and gravity.

Maybe the greatest contribution of suspension is in reminding the dancer to breathe. A motion carried on the breath has an organic quality, modulations, shadings, and nuances that enliven the dance and enhance the illusion that the dancer is as comfortable in the air as on the ground. Coupled with the concepts of succession and opposition, suspension links steps into flowing and logical phrases. Energy is imperceptibly gathered in the moment of suspension to be transformed into another motion and another and another, until the dance finally comes to an end.

12

ISOLATION

isolation = movement of one part of body

Isolation is both the most hidden and the most obvious of concepts. From the very first exercise of the barre, the concept is explored and tested. As with many other concepts, when it is applied correctly, the dancer is only aware of motion, moving freely from one position to another. However, when imperfectly mastered, the dancer becomes bound by his or her musculature; motions are tentative, and equilibrium is precarious.

different parts moving independent of the whole

Daniel Lewis describes several isolation exercises used by Limón at the beginning of class that involve moving just one part of the body; these isolations include rib and elbow, elbow and shoulder, and chest. He cautions the dancer to "Remember to feel the oppositional pulls in the body as you do the isolation exercises" (1984, 54).

use of opposit pulls

Although we have left the concept of isolation to the last, it is at the very foundation of ballet technique, which explicitly acknowledges that different parts of the body can move independently of the whole and that each has its own specific range of motion. Barre work directly addresses isolation through the practice of the ten exercises as each focus on a particular part of the body and its inherent range of motion, and this knowledge permeates the execution of all movements of the center vocabulary.

allowing us to see that each part has its own range of motion

In ballet technique, each joint is worked both to strengthen and to stretch the surrounding muscles. Because all joint are vulnerable, none more so than the weight-bearing joints of the legs, all barre exercises address the concern of building strength in the feet, knees, hip joints, and, of course, the spine. Isolation provides the focus to engage a particular part of the body, to test its range of motion, to strengthen it, and thereby to nurture its freedom.

The body can be likened to a family, whose the members are supportive of each other and act as a harmonious group, but still retain their individuality. In a functional body, the arm can move without the shoulder lifting, the leg can extend without a corresponding shift of the pelvis. It is possible because the limbs call on the inner strength of the muscles of the torso/spine, much as a family relies on the mutual trust and respect of its individual members.

Isolation gives the dancer the opportunity to discover the function, strength, weakness, range, and limitation of the different parts, so that each can move in a mutually supportive way, yet remain free. Isolation also highlights the interconnectedness between the different parts; how moving the arm affects the shoulder or moving the leg affects the pelvis. When the effect is recognized, it can be reshaped or altered, minimized or utilized to the full.

To support the notion of isolation, it is helpful to think of movement as occurring in the joint, and to think of shapes as created by placing the bones in specific positions. In other words, joints that are to be moved must be free. A locked joint does not easily yield and extra force becomes necessary to produce the shape, "Joints participate in the dialogue between movement and stillness, falling and balance. The space between the bones is the opening which allows mobility" (Olsen 1991, 113). The muscles will contract and flex naturally in response to the need to produce a specific shape, relying on the support of the inner musculature of the torso. Therefore, another benefit accrues from isolation: the muscular response for any motion will be commensurate with the effort needed to perform the action. To use the analogy of a family again, the father will not be fighting with the mother for control, but rather both will direct their energy toward a common goal.

To neophyte dancers, isolation often appears to be a *restriction* of motion instead of being perceived as *liberation*. This is a necessary stage to pass through in the process of gaining control and acquiring technique. However, the dancer eventually has to give up overt control and let the motions flow through the body. At that point, he/she begins to own the technique and finds freedom where there was constraint, joy where there was travail, and expressiveness where there was rote.

Isolation is a concept that is at the very core of early training. I realize I have made this claim for many of the concepts that we have discussed before. However, each time I have said that "this concept is at the very core of training," I believe it is true. We have to agree that there has to be more than one factor at the core of a complex technique such as ballet, and we have already explored how a variety of concepts can be applied to the same movement. Each teacher brings to the discipline a unique vision that is reflected in the emphasis given to one or another aspect of the technique. This accounts for the diversity of approaches in teaching ballet and ultimately in stylistic differences. However, the personal vision always needs to be conditioned by the precepts of the technique.

But to return to isolation, in their first class, children stand at the barre and stretch a leg. They are encouraged to move only the leg and not any other part of the body. With motions of the arms, the injunction is repeated. After much practice, they acquire the ability to move both arms and legs at the same time in harmonious motions. Within this process, the role of the supporting side in stabilizing the body in motion is explicitly acknowledged. In other words, if the base is not secure, the action from that base will be compromised.

The vocabulary at the early stages of training is necessarily very limited in order to lay the foundation for the acquisition of an untrammeled technique. The movements are practiced very slowly and in their simplest form, "The study of every movement must be first done very slowly, in the simplest, 'broken-down' form, with special attention to the torso, arms and head. Dividing a movement into its separate elements, it is necessary to keep in mind its final harmony and coordination of the entire body" (Kostravitskaya 1979, 16). This process is achieved in two ways: by isolating the working or acting part of the body from the supporting part, and by practicing steps in isolation from each other.

A few rules govern the physical isolations:

1. The working leg moves in isolation from the supporting side to foster freedom of motion and stability.
2. The shoulders are not raised when arms are lifted.
3. The pelvis remains placed and level when legs are lifted (with the exception of *arabesque* where a shift forward is allowed when the children are ready to do higher extensions).
4. With certain exercises such as *petits battements sur le cou de pied,* and *ronds de jambe en l'air,* the knee joint is worked in isolation from the thigh.
5. Equal attention is given to the working and supporting sides of the body.

In the same spirit, steps in the center are taught singly before they are linked to other steps. For example, a beginner class will practice a series of *glissades*, emphasizing each element:

1. Right leg in the back in fifth position; *plié* on both legs
2. *Dégagé:* sliding the back leg to *seconde* ending in *pointe tendue*, retaining *plié* on supporting leg
3. Pushing off the supporting leg to extend it to *pointe tendue*, causing weight to shift to the other leg, now in *plié*
4. Closing extended leg in fifth front so that the movement can be repeated to the same side

In the same class. *assemblés, sissonnes,* and *pas de chat* will be introduced with a similar break down.

Only after each of these steps is executed with some degree of accuracy can they be put together in an *enchaînement.* Initially *glissade* and *assemblé* will be practiced then later the *pas de chat* can be added. And so on through training when a new step is always learned in isolation before being put into combinations of steps (Paskevska 1990).

The same applies to the use of arms. In performing exercises at the barre, there is a very good reason why the arm is held in 2nd position. First, holding the position builds the muscles and connections to the back and pectoral muscles, second it allows the action of the arms to be isolated from the legs. In the center, the pathways for the arms are established with a variety of *port de bras* but not yet linked to action of the legs except in very simple exercises. When the pathways for the arms are established, they begin to be used with actions of the legs, again going from the simple to the complex. There are, of course, poses that require specific positions of the arms such as *arabesques* and *attitudes,* but even these rely on the precepts of pathways established earlier and can be taught in a consecutive way. For example, in a beginners's class, practicing *arabesques* will mean performing each move slowly: standing in fifth position (right leg front) the arms rise to 1st position then with a small *chassé,* the body turns to corner # 2, the back leg extends to *pointe tendue derrière,* the arms open from 1st position to the first *arabesque* (*allongé*) position, then the leg is lifted into *arabesque.* To finish the motion, the leg returns to *pointe tendue* and closes in fifth, the body faces front again as the arms open to 2nd, and are brought down to *bras bas.*

It is through the integration of the vocabulary that musculature is built; thus in order to build the kind of body that will be responsive, agile, and supple, it is necessary to perform the motions accurately and correctly. With each successive year of training, the development of the musculature and the connections established lead to an increased level of proficiency in the execution of the vocabulary. This physical progression is accompanied by heightened awareness of the intent of the motion. Concepts of alignment and isolation are in fact central to this development. The steps of the technique provide the tools to explore all concepts of motion, therefore mastering steps is important insofar as they are the overt manifestation of the concepts to be integrated. The process is somewhat circular: We do what we do to do what we do better.

The tools of the classical technique have been crafted over a long period of time, and are still being honed with each generation of new dancers. The dance field is led by choreographic innovations, but it is in the training years that bodies are molded and fashioned to cope with these innovations. These are the years when the instrument is built.

It is difficult to teach ballet as it should be taught, very, very slowly and with great attention to detail. It is difficult because the repetitions of simple motions may be boring for those who are not mature enough to value the task. It is also difficult because parents want results. They want their child to dance, which in a misguided way, they equate with learning steps. Finally it is difficult because commercial studios, per force, put their survival first and cater to an uninformed public that values glitz over substance, yet the developmental aspects of ballet training have yet to be seriously challenged by novel techniques or short cuts.

The situation is compounded by the propensity to teach children technique at too early an age. Before the age of seven or eight, children do not possess the physical and cognitive skills that will enable them to focus on the task of learning technique. There are many alternatives to ballet classes for very young children, dance activities that are fun, creative, and educational (see Chapter 13).

Most of the bad habits acquired through the early years of training stem from doing too much too soon. A child straining to achieve a high extension will do so at the expense of placement; the muscles designed to do the work being too weak will call on others for help, and a whole series of compensations will become part of the way the movement is perceived and performed. This process of compensation can also occur when the mechanics of a motion are not understood. One cannot expect young children to appreciate the ramifications of technique, therefore it falls upon the teacher to guide them until such age when they are developmentally ready to begin to analyze and connect. The goal of ballet training is to build a body that is capable of moving with ease, grace, power, and intent.

Isolation is at the very heart of the process of arriving at freedom of motion and continues to be relevant through a dancer's career as it encourages clarity and efficiency. In the daily class, the student learns the tenets of the technique embodied in the movements practiced and develops an ability to see and reproduce motions accurately.

Thus, the concept of isolation guides the student in acquiring a clean technique. The professional dancer, on the other hand, returns to her own base in the daily class and has the opportunity to reconnect with her physicality, thereby correcting misalignment and compensations that have arisen through performing.

3
The Practice

13

LAYING THE FOUNDATION

In this age of diversity and versatility, the need for a well-grounded technical base is extremely important. Technique can be very simply defined as the "how to" of any skill to be mastered. It is an acquired ability that takes time and effort congruent with the complexity of the skill to be learned. The acquisition of that base brings us inevitably to the developmental aspects of training. When ballet is taught with due consideration for the physical, cognitive, and intellectual development of children, the technique provides the vehicle to learn physical control through the acquisition of a vocabulary. Ballet technique reeducates the neuromuscular circuits in an initial and direct manner that has, so far, not been paralleled in other Western theatrical dance forms. Please do not throw the book down and stomp on it! There is supporting evidence for this claim.

Like most human endeavors that use the body as a vehicle, dance is both a physical and a neurological activity and as such its study has an impact on the brain. Research into the function of the brain has shown that "learning causes a dramatic increase in the number of synaptic connections between brain cells, resulting in a massive rewiring of the brain" (Kotulak 1990, 5). Research in the area of learning has further shown that the repetition of simple motions encourages the development of synaptic connections in the brain that augment our hard-wired movement vocabulary. Every time we learn a new skill, the process of integrating the unfamiliar motions results in the formation of new synaptic connections: "Using electron microscopy, (Black et al. 1990) showed that the number of synapses was greater in rats that learned new motor skills than in rats that exercised or had no opportunity for either learning or exercise" (Anderson, Alcantara, and Greenough 1996, 229). Greenough (1990) additionally indicates that repeating movements many times allows the new motions to be integrated into our automatic neuromuscular response circuits.

Ginsburg notes that "Organization...is the tendency common to all forms of life to integrate structures, both physical and psychological, into higher-order systems or structures" (1979, 18). Babies in the cradle wiggle, kick, and reach. Eventually they are able to crawl, then stand, and finally walk. A baby who did not crawl may have problems coordinating the oppositional (contralateral) aspects of locomotor activity and may even have some minor learning disabilities. It is a construct to separate the mind from the body; the physical impacts on the brain, just as the mind informs the body, "The mind is like the wind and the body like the sand; if you want to know how the wind is blowing, you can look at the sand" (Bainbridge Cohen 1993, 1). By practicing the hard-wired motions, we hone and refine innate skills. "The operation of the movement system is tremendously complex, calling upon the coordination of a dizzying variety of neural and muscular components in a highly differentiated and integrated fashion" (Gardner 1983, 210).

A beginner student in ballet will initially rely on the hard-wired circuits to perform the motions. But in a turned-out position, the muscles that are active in habitual locomotor motions may not be necessarily used in the same way. The addition of new information from an unfamiliar base results in a reeducation of the neuromuscular system; new information is added and integrated, and new synaptic connections are formed that permit more specialized communication between neurons. From this perspective, turn-out can be perceived as not merely an idiosyncratic demand stemming from an elitist dance form but a means to add locomotor options to our body/brain. "Each thought and behavior is embedded within the circuitry of the neurons and, according to one hypotheses, neuronal activity accompanying or initiating an experience persists in the form of reverberating neuronal circuits, which become more strongly defined with repetition" (Greenough 1990, 229).

The process of integrating movement vocabulary takes us from the general to the discrete or particular; a gradual honing in on the particulars of movements takes place through repetition of discrete movements— that is, a movement is learned in isolation from other movements until its specific form is assimilated. The students's experience goes from the general to an ever-increasing appreciation of the details inherent in specific steps or positions. First-year ballet students struggle to remember that the hip does not move, the knee is straight, and the toes point in a *battement tendu;* when they achieve a straight knee, they may forget to keep the back engaged. This simple motion takes years to perfect not only because synaptic connections take time to develop, but also because the dancer is forever improving one or another aspect of the movement. As some features of the movement become automatic, supported by clear commands from the brain, we have more freedom to think of more details to perfect.

This process suggests strongly that learning to dance requires an initial period of careful integration of the basic movements and postural habits that will allow a clean execution of the vocabulary. A complex combination of motions introduced before specialized synapses have been established denies the brain the opportunity to develop more differentiated synapses. Therefore, when the path and beginning and ending positions of a movement are not stressed, the information will be somewhat scrambled. It is like writing without punctuation or spaces between words:

itisdifficultandtimeconsummingtoreadsuchasentence.

The brain does not seem to register the individual components of a complex action and this results in an inability later on to easily make adjustments and improvements.

In my experience with new students at both the high school and college levels, those who have learned to dance by learning routines have greater difficulty in parsing movements—that is, seeing detail and correcting ingrained habits of motion—than those educated more conventionally within a conservative canon of ballet technique.

Learning to dance is not the same as learning steps. Steps are used initially to instill patterns of movement and later to test the proficiency of the neuronal connections through the evidence of the exactness with which they are performed. Through practice, in addition to the acquisition of a broadened vocabulary, several attributes that may be present in a nascent form are developed: a keen spatial awareness, response to rhythmic patterns, and an ability to see and therefore reproduce movement accurately. With practice and proficiency also comes the ability to distinguish the subtleties in movement, hear the rhythmic patterns more precisely, and perceive one's position in space in more nuanced ways, leading to analysis and judgment about the quality of one's response.

Developmentally, children are not ready to engage in the learning of technique before the age of seven (at the earliest), and waiting until the child is eight or even nine to start ballet technique is absolutely not too late. Jean Piaget (Miller 1983, 42) categorized children from two to seven years of age as being in the *preoperational stage*. He postulated that for a variety of developmental reasons, among them centrism (an inability to explore all aspects of an object, and an inability to attend to transformation), that the preoperational child is incapable of engaging in completely adult-like thought processes or integrating a series of events in terms of their relationships. This suggests that while children from three to seven years can benefit greatly from a creative or pre-ballet class, they are not ready for the regimentation and formalism of technique.

There are, however, available alternatives. In creative dance classes, children can hone their hard-wired functions, building dexterity in motions such as walking, twisting, skipping, galloping, and so forth. They acquire more control over their habitual motions; gain a sense of rhythm, and personal space and the space they share with others. They may also discover that their need for self-expression has an arena.

Howard Gardner states, "The preschool years are often described as a golden age of creativity, a time when every child sparkles with artistry" (1982, 86). Creative movement classes direct that creativity into meaningful motions. Much of the movement is mimetic; skipping like a rabbit, wriggling like a worm, etc. When I taught that age group, there were specific images, which were repeated in every class. The students's favorite was growing from a caterpillar into a butterfly: from the initial wriggling of the caterpillar through the spinning in making the cocoon, growing long legs and antennae, then pushing through and unfolding wings, to finally flying all over the room. The exercise not only provided opportunity for interpretation, but also introduced specific challenges, such as balancing, stretching, and contracting. My personal favorite game involved performing the particular motions of an animal or object that each child selected secretly. The other children tried to guess what was represented. In one class, among all the horses, cats, and flowers, one little girl assumed a rolled up position. She did not move. No one could guess what she was. Finally she declared, "I am a dot."

The opportunity for a child to explore her or his own creativity is an important developmental stage. If we are lucky, we may return to it in adulthood as a source of inspiration and direction for mature creativity.

When children have outgrown the preoperational stage and enter into the *concrete operations phase* they are ready to pursue the acquisition of technique. In Piaget's words:

> . . . at about the age of 7–8, certain changes take place in the modality of childish judgment which are in close relation to the appearance of a desire for a system and noncontradiction. This stage is characterized on the one hand by the beginnings of a positive observation of the external world, and on the other by an awareness of the implications contained in such reasoning as is connected with actual observation (1977, 114).

The exercises of the ballet barre and the introduction of some basic jumps provide at this time the perfect vehicle for augmenting, by the establishment of new synaptic connections, the innate vocabulary of motion in a sequential and logical manner, and capitalize on the child's developing ability to reproduce the motions observed.

In teaching ballet technique, several factors regulate the choices teachers make:

1. A *conceptual base* guides in the content of the class: the choice of combinations allows the students to experience specific concepts, such as alignment or opposition, in a variety of ways and in different contexts.
2. A *technical perspective* guides in the choice of material introduced. This addresses the level of the class and the degree of complexity the students can assimilate.
3. An *anatomical and aesthetic base* guides the corrections given to students. The teacher is constantly referencing the technical tenets and the physical/somatic expression of these tenets.

These factors become intellectually pertinent to students only when they have acquired a technical base, when they have matured in their ability to makes connections, and when they have enough vocabulary and enough control of their instrument to appreciate the underlying reasons for the execution of the technique. In other words, concepts cannot replace direct experience, but they can enhance understanding and inspire expressiveness.

Up to about the age of fourteen, learning to dance seems to be an outside-to-inside process. Students watch, see, and reproduce the movements and gestures of the teacher. To use Vygotsky's definitions, this process is an "interpersonal" one:

> Every function in the child's cultural development appears twice: first, on the social level, and later, on the individual level; first, *between* people (*interpsychological*), and then *inside* the child (*intrapsychological*). . . . *The transformation of an interpersonal process into an intrapersonal one is the result of a long series of developmental events* (1978, 57).

This seems to suggest that directive learning (watching and reproducing), as opposed to teaching systems that ". . . lead pupils to become agents in their own learning" (Smith-Autard 2002, 25), has a definite place in the education of a child. Smith-Autard suggests a model of learning dance that concentrates on creating, performing, and appreciating that relies on a movement vocabulary created by the students. This approach seems most applicable to creative movement classes, but fails to take into account that the early training in ballet primarily addresses the building of the body/mind. The acquisition of a vocabulary of motions essentially other than the habitual is the means used to fashion the instrument, because it precludes relying on an automatic response and leads to a conscious execution of gesture.

Thus, experiencing dance from inside is the next step in the development of dancers, the natural outcome of integrating the technique and recognizing one's limitations. In this context, the realization of limitations leads to a positive exploration of the possibilities of human physiology. Attempting to feel the movement as opposed to simply doing the movement motivates analysis and evaluation. The challenge is no longer simply to perform steps accurately, but to perform steps with more attention to detail, as well as more efficiency, and as a result, with less wear and tear on the body. It is at this point of training that the concepts that we have explored earlier in this book can refocus and guide the teacher and dancer to a heightened awareness of the inherent qualities of the vocabulary.

Many years ago I taught an elective ballet class at Indiana University that was open to the community. Two young students about fourteen years old, who had quite developed technical skills, also had a rather idiosyncratic way of placing and using the head, a sort of birdlike jerkiness. Some time later, I had occasion to see their teacher in class and realized that both girls had unconsciously integrated the teacher's way of using the head into their execution of the technique. This story illustrates that there is no critical or analytical evaluation at the early stages of learning; however the integration of information gathered during this period is vital because it inures specific physical habits, which can either serve future progress or detract from it. It is also a caution to teachers; as dancers we developed individual styles, as teachers we need to return to a clean technique lest we pass on our idiosyncrasies to our students. In the same context, some teachers rely on some powerful and mistaken ideas—like the traditional injunctions of "pull-up" and "tuck your tush"—which continue to have devastating results on alignment and freedom of movement in the joints. Contracting the musculature as opposed to engaging and energizing the body denies not only a clear experience of the technique but also prevents a true appreciation of one's body in relation to itself and the space in which it moves. In effect, the dancer loses the capacity to "feel" the real degree of effort necessary to perform the motion and the ability to move through space efficiently is compromised. There is no reason, given the plethora of information on child development, somatic techniques, and experiential anatomy, for the continued use of hazardous approaches to ballet training.

Appreciating all aspects of the technique—the mechanics of motion (how the body produces motions), the physics of motion (how the tenets of the technique facilitate the interaction between the body and the environment), and the aesthetics (line, attack, phrasing)—helps dancers maximize their potential and provides teachers with the tools to give pertinent corrections and directives to their pupils. Applying modern dance concepts to ballet technique encourages us to view the classical technique from a different vantage point. Applying the concepts is not the same as incorporating modern dance motions into the vocabulary; rather it is a probing into the properties of the classical technique and discovering its full breadth within its aesthetic.

14

EXERCISES OF THE BARRE

Turn-out is probably the most controversial aspect of ballet training. It came into practice when it became clear that the outward positioning of the feet, accompanied by the femoral rotation, provided more stability and was also shown to allow more mobility when the legs were raised. This usage was adopted from fencing positions. Like the steps of the technique it is based pragmatically on possibilities in the range of human motion.

Two factors are operative as soon as one intends to put the body in motion:

1. The range of motion and the properties of each joint (movement is determined by the range of motion of the joints)
2. The stabilization required to support the motion (no movement is possible without stabilization)

Thus ballet technique works within our physical limitations, but also aims to extend the range of motion while at the same time strengthening the vulnerable areas. When too much emphasis is given to stretching, the joints become vulnerable to misalignment and there is danger of injury. When too much emphasis is given to building strength, there is loss of flexibility through an unyielding build up of musculature. But when principles of motion are considered, as illustrated by the modern dance concepts that we have explored, the very nature of the classical vocabulary becomes evident and accessible. The ballet class can provide the perfect tool to navigate between the two extremes of strength and flexibility. The ten exercises of the barre are designed to address the mobility and strength of every joint of the body as within each exercise, there are stretching and strengthening components.

When alignment is the first priority in the transmission of the technique, then equal attention will be given to the use of the supporting and working sides. In other words, the emphasis will not solely be on performing a movement with the working leg, but equally on how the supporting side, indeed the whole body, is facilitating that motion. A distinction between alignment and placement must be made. *Alignment* describes the general configuration of the body: the head is balanced squarely on the atlantoaxial articulation, the shoulders are in direct line over the pelvis, the legs are rotated from the hip joint, the knees are in line both with the rotation of the femur and the heels, and the weight of the body is carried over the keystone of the feet. *Placement* refers more directly to the correct execution of movements within the classical aesthetic that cause the body to adjust to the shift of weight and recenter the mass over the support, and addresses more specifically the desired line of the classical technique.

The barre exercises provide the opportunity to experience motion incrementally: each exercise informs the next and impacts, more or less directly, on the correct execution of all exercises, as well as work in the center. All exercises work the hip joint to build mobility and strength, because this area is crucial in all motions. Some exercises address specifically one joint, such as the knee (*rond de jambe en l'air* and *petit battement sur le cou de pied*). The pelvic area is also engaged and active in all movements by virtue of the muscles passing through it that link the lower to the upper body and maintain the alignment of the spine (see Chapter 4). Moreover, all exercises address the concept of weight: the distribution of weight over the support and the transference of weight from one leg to the other. Some exercises also address the weight of limbs such as *battement balancé*.

The other modern dance concepts that we've discussed all come into play in the barre exercises. Isolation is central to the correct execution of all movements and impacts alignment (if the hip joint is not isolated, the motions will reverberate through the pelvic area and up and cause a series of compensations). Succession ensures the flow of movements and leads to an appreciation of pathways. Suspension brings into focus phrasing and the use of breath to support, emphasize, or modulate movements. Fall, potential and kinetic energy, and recovery and rebound all affect the quality of movements and share aspects with the preceding concepts such as phrasing, management of weight, and appreciation of pathways.

We look briefly at each exercise to determine their basic contribution to the acquisition of technique in terms of the modern dance concepts that they embody before exploring them within a focused structure of a lesson.

PREPARATORY PORT DE BRAS

From a *bras bas* position, the arm rises to 1st and opens *à la seconde.* The head follows the pathway of the arm, inclining slightly as the arm rises to 1st (with right arm the head inclines left) and turns toward arm as it opens *à la seconde.* Both motions, arm and head, have the property of insuring that the shoulder joint and the atlantoaxial connection are free of tension before directing attention to the legs.

PLIÉ *(BENDING)*

As the first exercise of the barre, *plié* is used for centering and establishing alignment and placement, as well as activating all the joints of the legs and introducing coordination between arms, head, and legs in the successive motion. *Pliés* foster vertical maintenance of the torso over the feet. Even as the knees bend, the feeling is one of stretching upward in opposition to the descent of the whole body. The motion is supported by the strength of the thighs, which preserve turn-out through opposition (knees reaching out in opposite directions.) *Pliés* also introduce isolation in its most basic manifestation; all the active joints are used freely, without being locked.

Pliés can be experienced as a gentle awakening of the whole body especially if the combination includes *cambrés.* Too often the body is like an old friend whom we take for granted. This exercise can put us back in touch with minute sensations and make us rejoice in our beingness.

BATTEMENT TENDU *(STRETCHING)*

Battement tendu is the first exercise that addresses weight transference: from fifth position, as the working leg begins to open to *pointe tendue,* the weight of the body shifts onto the supporting leg. The working leg stretches in opposition to the supporting leg, whose energy flows into the floor. The transfer of weight is minimal when starting from a fifth position, because the weight is already placed centrally and taking one leg away does not result in an overt movement, but rather a subtle redistribution of weight. (Performing *tendus* from first position is actually harder than from fifth or third positions, because it involves more of a shift onto the supporting leg). The weight on the supporting side is carried oppositionally through the leg into the floor and through the pelvis as it maintains alignment (maintaining is best experienced as a motion moving away from the gesture leg).

Furthermore, the weight is carried over the center of the supporting femoral head as it nestles in the acetabular cavity, and must not shift to the greater trocanter. Sliding off the femur is generally referred to as "sitting." It is important to preserve the integrity of the supporting joint, because sinking into the joint impinges upon mobility and affects negatively the ability to maintain turn-out. Even though the adjustment of weight is slight, it is nevertheless significant because it conditions the body to recognize the new placement and find it again when the leg is lifted off the floor or when landing from a jump. In effect, the correct execution of *tendu* anticipates all motions that require the leg to be lifted off the floor, be it in a low or a high extension. By keeping the torso, including the pelvic area, aligned an awareness of the degree of weight transfer necessary in higher extensions is developed.

As the first exercise that addresses a shifting of weight, however slight, *tendu* fosters an awareness of center and the reorganization of weight around the axis. When done slowly, it takes on a feline quality, a cat stretching a paw, and when performed at a faster tempo it sparkles with energy.

BATTEMENT JETÉ *(THROWING)*

Jeté differs from *tendu* in its dynamics; although the height is controlled, the motion has the feeling of being thrown. The action instills awareness of intent in limiting the extension and tests the ability of the body to preserve verticality on the supporting side while the working leg is engaged in a more forceful movement.

In this exercise, the concept of opposition complements those of fall and recovery. After the initial extension to forty-five degrees, the leg falls back into fifth and recovers to an open position. The fully stretched, engaged leg does not need further muscular contractions to bring it back to fifth; gravity acting on the weight of the leg will do that. Additionally, as with any movement that closes in fifth, the weight of the body rests on both feet every time the working leg returns to fifth. The weight-shift although minimal nevertheless nurtures dexterity: the ability to change weight rapidly as motions demand. As mentioned earlier, performing both *tendus* and *jetés* at breakneck speed does not foster dexterity; rather the ability to move fast is developed through the correct execution of these movements, which includes putting one's weight on both feet when the working leg returns to fifth position. When the tempo is too fast, students cannot transfer their weight onto both legs in fifth or release the instep, which prevents them from truly feeling contact with the floor.

As an aside, ballet technique takes into consideration that whenever a leg is extended off the floor, the body moves away from the direction of that extension. The shift is necessary to accommodate the weight of the lifted leg. However, the technique also aims to minimize the shift to achieve the desired line and builds the inner musculature to support verticality. Gripping outside muscles, to perform the motion or preserve equilibrium, is not an option; it denies experiencing the inner musculature. In this minimizing process, the body becomes aware of exactly how little or how much shifting is necessary to maintain equilibrium. The awareness of equilibrium, in turn, fosters the ability to perceive and return from disequilibrium. As Doris Humphrey stated, dance happens between fall and recovery. This is what makes dance exciting, the ever-present danger of falling and returning from the edge.

Battement jeté, while sharing some of the dynamics of a fast *battement tendu,* is a more emphatic gesture; the working leg disengages with éclat, suspends for a second (without gripping), to return purposefully back to the closed position.

ROND DE JAMBE PAR TERRE
(CIRCLING OF THE LEG ON THE FLOOR)

Rond de jambe par terre introduces a rotation in the hip joint, which anticipates all movements that utilize rotation. The concepts of opposition between the supporting and the working legs and alignment of the body are again pertinent. Additionally, the concept of isolation is now applied to a circular motion. The rotation within the hip joint of the working leg is possible only if that joint is free, not contracted. The freedom within the hip joint ensures that the motion of the working leg is isolated from the pelvis and therefore does not result in a sympathetic rotation of the pelvis that inevitably transfers to the supporting hip joint. Again, sitting into the supporting side impacts negatively on alignment, impinges on the mobility of the joint and its ability to maintain *turn-out,* and usually results in an unwelcome and unnecessary wiggle. And, it cannot be stressed enough: turn-out, both on the working and supporting sides, at all times, needs to be perceived as a movement and not a position.

When the leg travels from front to back *(en dehors),* the thigh is felt to be opening, and after the extension to the back, the inner thigh, with an aligned heel, leads the motion through first position. When traveling from back to front (*en dedans*) the inner thigh again leads the motion in harmony with the rotation in the hip joint, anticipating the turned out arrival of the leg to the side then the front. Through first position, the toes remain aligned to the heel to preserve turn-out.

Because the movement is performed with the toes on the floor, that is, in the lowest extension, there is no pelvic shift during the *ronds par terre*. Nevertheless the exercise, by establishing verticality on the supporting leg, and practicing the smooth rotation of the hip joint, prepares for all motions that require the body to adapt and remain balanced, even when the working leg lifts in high extensions and moves from one position to another.

BATTEMENT FONDU *(MELTING)*

Battement fondu addresses the concepts of alignment, opposition, and suspension. It develops coordination between the two legs as the working leg unfolds to an extension and the supporting leg straightens out from its *plié*. It develops tensile strength and balance and can be performed to *à terre* position from the *cou de pied* or to a full extension from a *retiré*. In its slow unfolding, it promotes awareness of the internal relationship between body and limbs and the adjustment necessary when the leg is lifted above ninety degrees. It suspends in the extension before returning to *retiré*. *Fondu* also anticipates the positions used in *adagio*.

Principles of *épaulement* can be easily introduced and practiced with *battement fondu*. Because the tempo is usually slow, it gives the opportunity to explore the spiraling of the spine in a very controlled manner.

BATTEMENT FRAPPÉ *(HITTING, STRIKING)*

Battement frappé is a percussive motion that includes the concepts of potential and kinetic energy and recovery. *Frappé* owes its name to the quality of the thrust and not to the action of hitting the floor. From a *cou de pied* position, the leg extends forcefully to a fully stretched position then returns to the *cou de pied*. From the initial preparation, which places the working foot on the ankle of the supporting leg, potential energy is ready to be released in the outward thrust. The return to the supporting ankle is more like recovery than like rebound; there is no additional tensing of muscles necessary.

Throughout the sequence, turn-out is maintained and the action is primarily experienced through the flexion of the knee and ankle joints. Performing the motion with a flexion at the ankle joint in the *cou de pied* position, instead of a fully pointed foot throughout, encourages a muscular connection to be made and maintained between the turn-out at the hip joint and the *turn-out* of the lower leg all the way to the heel. This connection fosters speed in jumps and the ability to execute multiple beats in *petite batterie* vocabulary.

ROND DE JAMBE EN L'AIR
(CIRCLING THE LEG IN THE AIR)

Besides encouraging control of the working hip joint and alignment on the supporting side, *rond de jambe en l'air* includes isolation in the knee joint, and suspension while the lower working leg is circling and opposition as it straightens. Further, it releases kinetic energy in the initial thrust from the floor to ninety degrees. *Rond en l'air* concentrates on the action of the knee joint in its limited capacity to rotate in isolation from the thigh. "Possible actions at the knee joint are flexion and extension, plus the possibility of slight rotation when the knee is flexed" (Fitt 1988, 137). The rotation also strengthens the muscles that support the integrity of the knee. It is not possible to rotate the knee while the weight of the body rests on the legs, therefore the positioning of the leg *en l'air* is a precondition for the execution of this motion, and the thigh does not move during the action of the lower leg,

DÉVELOPPÉ AND GRAND ROND DE JAMBE EN L'AIR
(UNFOLDING AND BIG CIRCLING
OF THE LEG IN THE AIR)

Alignment, placement, opposition, succession, and suspension are again tested and experienced with *développés*. But managing the weight of the extended leg and concomitant adjustments in the pelvic area are its primary features. The movement's action is a little different depending on the direction of the extension. To the front, once the leg has been lifted to a high *retiré*, the inner thigh and foot lead the motion outward to the full extension. The spine remains straight and the pelvis does not tuck under. The iliapsoas muscles carry the weight of the leg. To the side, the thigh is lifted further upward from the *retiré* position before the leg begins to unfold; again the inner thigh supports the extension. The pelvis tilts imperceptibly sideways to allow for extensions above 90 degrees, but remains centered over the supporting hip joint. The tilting does not anticipate the final position, rather the pelvis responds to and is guided by the leg in the degree of the adjustment as the movement proceeds; furthermore, the pelvis only tilts sideways not under. To the back, the thigh again leads the unfolding and the pelvis tilts forward in response. Similarly to extensions to the side, the pelvis responds to the height of the leg and does not anticipate that height by tilting prematurely. Utilizing the concepts of opposition and suspension prevents the quads from bunching up specifically in extension to the front and side.

In *grand rond de jambe en l'air*, there is a very subtle and slow release of kinetic energy supported by a feeling of opposition, suspension, and succession. The movement follows the same pathway as *ronds par terre*, but the height of the leg necessitates an adjustment of weight and pelvic repositions. The mass or weight of the body adjusts smoothly and successively as the working leg moves *en dehors* from front to side to back or reverses in the *en dedans* motion. When performed *en dehors*, the pelvis adjusts and tilts only in response to the position of the leg, never anticipating the next position on its path. With *en dedans*, the pelvis responds immediately to the rotating action of the leg by returning to an upright position from its forward tilt in *arabesque*. The pelvis then remains placed while the leg concludes the rotational circling (from side to front). Proximal initiation and control in the hip joint is central to the correct execution of the *en dedans* motion. However, at ninety degrees, the muscles of the torso, and notably the *psoas*, hold the leg up; therefore the quads, although engaged, do not bunch. This process is greatly enhanced by the feeling of opposition; that is, the leg, secure in its connection within the acetabular cavity, is felt to reach outward in opposition to the standing leg.

PETIT BATTEMENT SUR LE COU DE PIED (LITTLE BEATING ON THE ANKLE)

Petit battement sur le cou de pied fosters the ability to isolate the joints of the legs. The hip and ankle joints are kept placed; that is the femur maintains *turn-out*, the thigh does not move, and the ankle joint holds the semi-flexed position that allows the foot to wrap around the supporting ankle. The action is entirely limited to the knee joint. In a small swinging action (like a pendulum), the heel of the working foot hits alternatively the back and front of the supporting ankle. The working knee joint conforms to the concept of recovery while the stabilizing joints (hip and ankle) store potential energy, which is released through the swing of the leg.

This motion is even more directly linked to *petite batterie* than the *frappé*. Like *frappé*, it encourages the connection between the inner thigh and the heel, but anticipates more precisely the action of the legs in *entrechats* by building neuromuscular patterns for the action of the inner thighs and heels in their action of bypassing each other during the jump. (This patterning does not occur when *petit battement* is executed with a fully pointed foot.)

GRAND BATTEMENT *(BIG BEATING)*

Grand battement tests the ability to preserve alignment (retaining verticality) and placement (maintaining turn-out, adapting to the necessary shifts, returning to center when closing in fifth). Additionally, kinetic energy is released as the foot pushes off the floor and the leg thrusts upward. Similar, but more dramatically than in *battement jeté*, weight, fall, and opposition are active concepts during the descent of the leg. The weight of the leg brings it down; giving in to gravity is the property of fall. The lengthening associated with opposition prevents further and unnecessary muscular contractions from occurring.

PORT DE BRAS

Any discussion of barre exercises needs to include the role of the arms, but we begin by addressing the subject from the developmental perspective.

The classical position of the arms demands that the humerus be rotated inwards while the lower arm is rotated slightly outward (in opposition to the upper arm). The elbows are never entirely straight, which helps to preserve the characteristic slight curve of the arm. There is no tension either in the elbow or the wrist (these joints are never locked), and in 2nd position the hand continues the slightly drooping line of the arm (the hand is a little below the shoulder line). The palm of the hand faces front but is somewhat hidden by the thumb angled across it (directed toward the middle finger); the fingers are separated. The middle finger is lower than the others and all are placed in a soft curve (see Figure 25).

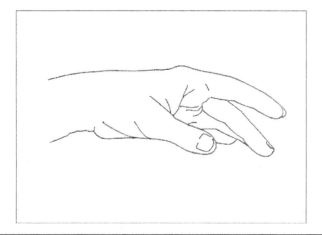

Figure 25

There are a couple of training methods to ensure that the hand ends in the correct position; Preobrajenskaya made her beginning students hold together the tips of the second finger and thumb (forming an O) with the other fingers also curved. After a couple of years, she allowed a release of contact, at which point the hand naturally relaxed into a curved position with fingers appropriately placed. Another method makes the contact by placing the thumb at the middle of the second finger. This positioning is more suitable for boys, because it encourages a less pronounced curve of the fingers.

During the initial years of training, the connection between the arm and the head is learned with the first *port de bras* (from *bras bas,* the arm lifts to 1st then opens to 2nd). At the barre, the arm is generally held in 2nd position. Holding the arm in 2nd position is a very important component in the development of the musculature of the torso and encourages awareness of the connection between the upper and lower halves of the body. Holding the arm in position instills the habit of using the arms independently from the legs, fostering cooperation but not dependency. In the center, *ports de bras* are practiced in isolation from the legs until the positions and pathways are established, then they are linked to steps.

Academically, there is no more license in the use of arms than there is in the execution of steps. Academic/traditional usage of arms facilitates and enhances motions and positions, thus using arms in a specific fashion to accompany specific steps is founded on the same principles as those governing the body, i.e., opposition and weight in held positions, succession and suspension in slow *port de bras,* potential and kinetic energy, and recovery and rebound in *pirouettes* and jumps are all active concepts in the use of arms.

The arms obey the laws of opposition, for example, in the *effacé* and *croisé* positions, the opposite arm to the front leg is in 5th position; the other arm in 2nd (4th *en haut* position of the arms). With *arabesques,* the position of the arms actually determines which *arabesque* is performed: first *arabesque* requires the same arm as the standing leg to be in *allongé devant.* If the opposite arm is brought forward, the position becomes *épaulée* or second *arabesque.* And third *arabesque* is characterized by both arms in *allongé devant* (Paskevska 1981).

The placement of the arms also acknowledges the backward pull of gravity; with the exception of some *arabesques,* the arms are never placed behind the shoulders. In most steps of the *petit allegro* vocabulary, the arms are used to ensure that the distribution of weight provides a safe and balanced landing: one arm is placed in 1st position to emphasize the distribution of weight on the landing leg in steps such as *petits jetés* (see

Figure 12). Similarly, in steps like *sissonnes*, the arm emphasizes the maintenance of the weight over the front leg by bringing to 1st position the same arm as the leg closing front at the conclusion of the movement.

While in *adagio* the arms help preserve balance and fluidity, in big jumps they maximize the push off the floor and again help in maintaining balance in the air. All these rules and regulations serve to place the whole body in an optimal position to perform specific motions and steps, and are central to the acquisition of a solid technique.

CONCLUSION

The exercises of the barre lay the foundation for the execution of virtually every motion in the vocabulary of the technique. They establish the relationship between the supporting and acting sides and the pathways for moving from one position to another. Further, they condition the body to respond to weight transference and set degrees of attack or the quality of the disengagement from the floor. They also allow an exploration of the range of motions and the possibility of subsequently, with practice, extending these boundaries.

15

INTRODUCTION TO THE CLASS

Concepts are not movements; rather, they act as mental initiators and address the quality of motions. As we have seen, in any one exercise there are usually several concepts that either facilitate the execution of the exercise or give it a specific quality. This makes it difficult to isolate just one concept as the sole topic for a given class. For example, if we choose to address recovery and rebound, we will, perforce, have concerns also with weight and fall and even with opposition and succession. The teacher then decides which quality to bring to the fore, and will illustrate it specifically by devising exercises at the barre and combinations in the center that will allow a direct experience of the concepts or quality in a range of applications.

It is also good to remember that while ballet terminology is descriptive of the qualities inherent in the motions and allows us to access the intent of the exercise or combination; the use of modern dance concepts deepens the experience and serves to enhance the traditional ballet nomenclature.

As the class below illustrates, exercises and steps of the center can embody specific concepts and help enhance the experience of motions. The emphasis on one aspect or another of a movement is the choice of the teacher and is further dependent upon the level of the class. If, for example, the class has been working on becoming more aware of the lyrical quality of movements, then suspension, succession, and opposition will be highlighted. Conversely, if pushing off the floor needs attention, then recovery, rebound, and weight can be stressed.

Technique utilizes the knowledge of our body and the givens of the space we occupy to produce the optimum way of dealing with the issues and possibilities inherent in the material at our disposal—that is, the vocabulary. Ballet technique is founded on possibilities. In a very real sense, people stand between their environment and their inventions. We translate the world around us and reinvent it in our creations. Just as the sculptor must understand the properties of his material, be it wood or stone, dancers must understand how the body works and responds to its environment. In this respect, a familiarity with somatic techniques can also inform one's understanding of ballet. However, in the process of incorporating ideas from other forms, one has to remain aware of the ultimate goal of the technique one is teaching and how the technical skills imparted to the students will be used.

Modern dance approaches movement from a different aesthetic than classical ballet, but the concepts explored are relevant to all dance and provide the tools to address quality of motion in a direct and clear manner. Even while ballet in many ways sublimates some of the concepts such as fall and weight, they are nevertheless inescapable components of technique.

A sample, advanced-level class follows with suggested concept qualities linked to specific movements. However, I do not pretend to have exhausted the possibilities and these suggestions should not preclude mentioning other concepts when applicable. Additionally, alignment, awareness of center, isolation, and weight (fall always includes weight) are implicitly present in all motions.

THE CLASS

Barre

Pliés 4/4 or 3/4 (In second, first, fourth, and fifth)
Note: first *port de bras*: from *bras bas* arm lifts to 1st position and opens to 2nd. Areas of isolation: hip, knee, and ankle and shoulder joints.

1 grand *plié*. *Cambré* starting to the side toward the barre, continuing, circling down, then up to upright (rolling successively up), arm finishing in 2nd. *Cambré* back arm in 2nd, palm up, head turned to hand. In second, first, fourth, and fifth positions. (Cleo Nordi always started *pliés* in second position.)

Movement	Concept
Preparation: first *port de bras* to 2nd position	Succession
1–4: *Grand plié*	Opposition (spine extends upward. Thighs reach outwards).

1–4: *Cambré* side.	Opposition (legs reach into the floor. Arm reaches outward and sideways towards the barre). Succession.
1–4: *Cambré* around body continues forward and finishes upright. The arm leads the circular succession motion and ends in 2nd position.	Succession Fall, (forward). Recovery to vertical position
1–4: *Cambré* back. Arm in 2nd, palm up, head turned toward arm. Return to upright Repeat in all positions.	Opposition. Succession to vertical

Battements Tendus 4/4

Areas of isolation: Hip, ankle, shoulder joints.

    A. 1 *tendu devant* to open position, *plié* in fourth, point and close in fifth. 1 *tendu devant, plié* on supporting leg, *demi rond de jambe par terre* to side close in front. B. 1 *tendu en croix* (front, side, back, side) closing in front after the last one. Repeat A to the side ending the *rond de jambe* in *pointe tendue derrière*. Instead of closing in fifth after extension to the back bring leg through first position to *devant* then to *seconde*. Eight *tendus* to side into first last one closing back. Repeat from A beginning *derrière*.

    Arm comes to 1st position in *pliés* in fourth and second and does a full *port de bras* (*en dehors*: through 1st to 5th, opening to 2nd. *En dedans*: from 2nd to 5th through 1st (*bras bas* to 2nd) during the *tendus en croix* and the quick *tendus* into first (*en dehors* when exercise starts front, then *en dedans* when reversing).

Movement	Concept
Preparation: first *port de bras* to 2nd. A.	Succession
1: *Tendu devant,*	Succession stretching to pointe *tendue.* Opposition between standing and working legs.
And 2: *Demi plié* in fourth position,	Fall.
3 and 4: *Pointe tendue* and close in fifth,	Recovery. Opposition.
5–6: *Tendu devant* and *plié* on supporting leg	Opposition (*tendu*). Fall (*plié*)

7: Stretch supporting leg in *demi rond* to side,	Recovery. Succession.
8: close fifth front	Weight

B.

1–8 One *tendu en croix*. Close front after the last one.	Opposition and succession.

Repeat A in *seconde* through 7

8: from *pointe tendue derrière*, pass through first and *rond de jambe* (*en dehors*) to *seconde*.

1–8 Eight *tendus* in *seconde* closing in first, with *port de bras en dehors*.	Opposition
Close last one fifth *derrière*,	Succession

Repeat from A through B beginning *derrière* and with *port de bras en dedans*, during *tendus* into first.

Battements Jetés   2/4

Areas of isolation: hip, knee, ankle joints.

A. Two *jetés devant* closing in fifth. One *jeté* to fourth position to *demi plié* on both legs. Transfer weight onto front leg extending back leg in low extension derrière. *Demi plié* in fourth and transfer weight to back leg, front leg in low extension *devant* (the extensions can also be done onto *demi pointe*). *Balancé* through first to *derrière* and close in the back. Repeat starting *derrière*.

B. Two *jetés* to *seconde* (closing back then front). One *jeté* to seconde into *demi plié*. Transfer weight onto original working leg then back again to original supporting leg through another *demi plié*, two *jetés* closing back then front. Repeat B to *demi plié* in *seconde* (as preparation) *pirouette en dehors* closing in the back.

Repeat from A. *Pirouette* will be *en dedans* and closes in front.

Movement	Concept
Preparation: first *port de bras* to 2nd position.	Succession.
A.	
And 1 and 2: Two *jetés devant* into fifth.	Opposition. Kinetic energy.
And 3: One *jeté* into fourth position *demi plié*,	Fall.
And 4: Transfer to front leg, back leg extended *derrière* (low *en l'air*)	Rebound. Opposition.
5–6: Transfer to back leg through *demi-plié* in fourth extending the front leg in *devant*.	Fall. Rebound.
	Opposition.

7 and 8: *Balancé* through first position to *derrière*, close in fifth.	Weight. Fall. Recovery.
Repeat A in reverse, starting *derrière*.	
B.	
And 1 and 2: Two *jetés* to *seconde* closing back then front.	Opposition. Kinetic energy.
And 3 and 4: One *jeté* to *seconde* to *demi plié*, transfer to original working leg, other leg extended to low *seconde*.	Opposition. Fall. Rebound.
5 and 6: Return to original supporting leg through *demi plié* in second. Working leg in low extension.	Fall. Rebound. Suspension.
7 and 8: Two *jetés* closing fifth back then front.	Opposition.
Repeat from count 1 to 3 (to side with *demi plié* in second) Arm in 1st position.	Fall.
5 and 6: *Pirouette en dehors*	Kinetic energy. Suspension.
7 and 8: Close in fifth back.	Recovery.
Repeat A and B beginning *derrière* ending with *pirouette en dedans.*	

Ronds de jambe par terre 3/4

Areas of isolation: hip joint rotation, knee, ankle, spine

Four *ronds de jambe en dehors.* Lift leg in front and *tombé en avant* into deep fourth position (onto working le.g., other leg extended *derrière.*) *Cambré* forward. Straighten supporting leg, *cambré* back. *Temps lié* to return to original supporting leg, Four *ronds de jambe en dedans.* Lift leg in *arabesque* and *tombé en arrière* to *demi plié,* then straighten supporting leg, other leg extended in front (*pointe tendue*). *Demi plié* with *cambré* forward. Straighten supporting leg, *Cambré* back. *Temps lié* to return to original supporting leg, Arms are in 2nd position through *ronds* and do a *port de bras en dehors* with *cambrés.* The exercise can be repeated and finish with a *piqué* into *arabesque* to balance.

(Numbers (i.e., 1–4) indicate bars not beats)

Movement	Concept
1–4 Preparation: first *port de bras* to 2nd position. *Demi plié* to *pointe tendue devant, demi rond de jambe* to *seconde.*	Succession. Opposition.
1–4: Four *ronds de jambe en dehors*	Succession. Opposition.

5–8: Leg lifts *devant* with *relevé.* Suspension. Fall.
   Tombé en avant into deep lunge in
   fourth position back leg Opposition.
   stretched and toes *pointed à terre.*
1–3: *Cambré forward.* Opposition. Succession. Fall.
4: Body returns to vertical. Recovery. Opposition.
   Supporting leg straightens. Suspension. Succession.
   (Arm in 5th)
5–7: *Cambré* back. As body returns to Opposition. Succession.
   vertical arm opens to 2nd
And 8: *Temps lié* to *pointe tendue* Fall. Recovery. Succession.
   devant (onto original supporting leg)
1–4: Repeat *ronds en dedans* Succession. Opposition.
5–8: Lift leg to *derrière* with *relevé* Suspension. Fall. Opposition.
   to *demi pointe.*
   Tombé into *demi plié*, front leg in
   pointe tendue devant.
   Straighten supporting leg Recovery.
1–3: *Cambré* forward. Arm moves Opposition. Suspension.
   to 5th with *demi plié* on Succession.
   supporting leg
4–5: Body returns to vertical. Opposition. Succession.
   Supporting leg straightens. Recovery.
6–7: *Cambré* back, arm extending to Opposition. Suspension.
   allongé devant, Succession.
And 8: *temps lié* onto original Fall. Succession. Recovery.
   supporting leg. Working leg *derrière.* Suspension.

Battements fondus   3/4

Areas of isolation: hip, knee, ankle joints
   Note: Arm performs first *port de bras* with each *fondu.*
   One *fondu devant. Tombé en avant,* other leg in *arabesque. Fouetté
en dehors* ending facing other side with working leg *devant.* With new
working leg: one *fondu croisé devant,* one *fondu croisé derrière,* one
fondu to seconde. Plié and *relevé* in *retiré* with half turn *en dehors* to
return to original side. *Coupé* and extend original working leg in *arabesque, demi plié* on supporting leg. Repeat beginning *derrière* with
fouetté and *relevé* in *retiré en dedans* and final extension in high *devant*
position.
   Entire sequence can be repeated on half *pointe.* Exercise can be performed either with forty-five degrees extensions or to ninety degrees.

Numbers (i.e., 1–4) indicate bars not beats.

Note: when *coupé* occurs following the extension the working leg closes in fifth and the weight is transferred to the original working leg without passing through a *retiré* position.

Movement	Concept
Preparation : first *port de bras* to 2nd position. *dégagé* to *seconde*.	Succession. Opposition.
1–2: *Fondu devant*.	Succession. Opposition. Suspension.
3–4: *Tombé en avant*, other leg in *arabesque*.	Fall. Opposition.
relevé in *arabesque* and *fouetté en dehors*,	Rebound.
facing other side leg in extension *devant*.	Suspension. Opposition.
5–6: (Facing other side) *fondu* to *croisé devant*.	Fall. Opposition. Suspension.
7–8: *Petit battement* and *fondu* to *croisé derrière*.	Opposition. Suspension.
1–2: *Fondu* to *seconde*	Opposition. Suspension.
3–4: *Plié relevé*, with leg in *retiré* half turn *en dehors* to face original side.	Rebound. Suspension.
5–8: Soft *coupé*. Extend back leg in *arabesque*. Supporting leg in *demi plié*.	Fall. Opposition. Suspension.

Repeat *en dedans*:

Fouetté is *en dedans* ending with extension in *arabesque*. Half turn in *retiré* is *en dedans*, ending extension in high *devant* position.

Note: *en dehors* and *en dedans* in the *fouetté* refer to the turn, i.e., *en dehors* toward working leg, *en dedans* away from the working leg,

Battements frappés   2/4

Areas of isolation: hip, knee, ankle joint

Five *frappés devant*. *Tombé dessus* to fifth other leg on *cou de pied derrière*, arm in 1st, head angled over arm. *Coupé dessous, dégagé devant* with original working leg. Arm in 2nd. Bring leg to *cou de pied*. Five *frappés* to *seconde*. *Tombé dessus*. *Coupé, dégagé* to *seconde*. Repeat to *derrière* and *seconde* (*en croix*): the *coupés* are now *dessous* with head angled toward working side shoulder. Repeat on *demi pointe*. Sequence can end with *fouetté en dehors* and a balance in *attitude*.

Movement	Concept
Preparation: *pointe tendue seconde* with first *port de bras* to 2nd position	Succession. Opposition.
1–5: Five *frappés devant*	Kinetic energy.
6–: *Tombé* (to fifth), onto original working leg other leg in *cou de pied* position *derrière*, arm in 1st	Fall.
7–: *Coupé dessous. Degagé en l'air devant* with original working leg, Arm in 2nd.	Kinetic energy. Suspension.
8–: Bring leg to *cou de pied*.	Recovery.
1–5: Five *frappés* to the side.	Kinetic energy.
6–: *Tombé dessus*, other leg on *cou de pied derrière*. Arm in 1st.	Fall.
7–8: *Coupé dessous. Dégagé seconde en l'air.*	Kinetic energy. Suspension.
Arm in 2nd. Return to *cou de pied*.	Recovery.
Repeat *derrière* and *seconde* with *tombé dessous* and *coupé dessus*. Repeat on *demi pointe*.	

Ronds de jambe en l'air and adagio   3/4

Areas of isolation: hip, knee joints
Four *ronds de jambe en l'air en dehors. Passé* to *développé effacé devant. Relevé* and *tombé* (away from the barre) to second *arabesque. Passé* to *développé écarté devant. Demi plié, piqué* (toward the barre) to extension in *seconde.* Close in fifth back. Repeat *en dedans.* (*Passé* to *développé effacé derrière. Tombé* to *effacé devant. Passé* to *écarté derrière.*) Numbers (i.e., 1–4) indicate bars not beats.

Movement	Concept
Preparation: first *port de bras* to 2nd.	Succession.
1–4: Four *ronds de jambe*.	Kinetic energy. Suspension.
5–6: *Passé* to *développé devant effacé* on *demi plié* with first *port de bras* to 2nd, head turned toward barre.	Suspension. Succession. Opposition.
7–8: *Relevé*, and *tombé* to second *arabesque*.	Rebound. Fall. Opposition.

1–4: *Retiré, passé* to high *écarté devant.* Succession. Suspension.
5–7: *Demi plié* and *piqué,* towards barre, Kinetic energy.
original working leg in high *seconde.* Suspension.
8: Close fifth back.
Repeat *en dedans.* Head is turned toward
barre in *effacé devant* and away in
effacé derrière.

Petits battements sur le cou de pied 6/8
Area of isolation: knee joint

Fourteen counts of *petits battements. Dégagé* to *seconde,* with *demi plié* on supporting leg. *Relevé* on *demi pointe.* Sixteen counts of *petits battements battus* (in front) with *port de bras en dehors.* Repeat sequence with *battements battus* in the back and *port de bras en dedans.* Finish exercise with *pied à la main* to stretch out muscles of the hip joint.

Movement	Concept
Preparation: *dégagé* to *seconde* placing foot on the *cou de pied devant* with first *port de bras.*	Succession.
Arm in *bras bas* during *petits battements.*	
1–14: *Petits battements sur le cou de pied.*	Rebound.
15–16: *Dégagé* to *seconde* on *demi plié,* and *relevé* on half *pointe*	Opposition. Rebound.
1–16: *Petits battements battus devant.*	Rebound.
Port de bras en dehors.	Succession.
Repeat *en dedans.*	

Grands battements 2/4
Areas of isolation: hip, knee, ankle joint

Two *grands battements devant.* One *grand battement* to *tombé en avant,* other leg extended *derrière. Piqué* back to original supporting leg with working leg doing a *grand battement devant.* Closing in fifth. Repeat *en croix.* (*Grand battement* preceding the *tombé* can also be done with a *relevé* to *demi pointe.*)

Movement	Concept
Preparation: *Port de bras* to 2nd.	Succession.
1–4: Two *grands battements devant.*	Kinetic energy. Fall. Opposition.

5–6: One *grand battement. Tombé*   Fall. Opposition.
   en avant into *demi plié* with other
   leg extended *derrière.*
7–8: *Piqué* onto original supporting leg   Rebound. Suspension.
   with *grand battement* (original   Opposition.
   working leg)
Close in fifth.
Repeat *en croix.*

Center

Port de bras and pirouettes   4/4

Chassé en avant to *pointe tendue croisée derrière. Temps lié* to back leg,
front leg *pointe tendue croisée devant. Détourné en dedans,* lifting the
working leg into second *arabesque croisée. Demi plié* working leg *sur le
cou de pied derrière, pas de bourrée en tournant en dehors* ending *sur le
cou de pied derrière* on other leg, *Pas de bourrée en tournant en dehors*
ending in fourth position *croisée* (preparation). *Pirouettes en dehors*
closing fifth back. Repeat to other side.

Movement	Concept
Preparation: fifth position right leg in front. First *port de bras* to 2nd position	Succession.
1–2: *Chassé en avant* to *pointe tendue derrière croisée.*	Succession. Suspension. Opposition
Arms to *bras bas* rising to fifth.	Succession. Fall. Recovery.
3–4: *Temps lié* onto back leg,	Succession.
front leg in *pointe tendue devant croisée. Port de bras en dedans*	Opposition. Suspension.
through 1st position, *bras bas* to 2nd.	Fall. Recovery. Suspension.
5–8: *Détourné en dedans*	Opposition.
(away from front leg which finishes in the back.) Lifting to second	Succession. Suspension. Opposition.
arabesque.	
Arms pass through 1st to *allongé* in second *arabesque croisée.*	Fall. Recovery. Opposition.
1–2: *Demi plié,* back leg *sur le cou de pied derrière, pas de bourrée*	Fall. Recovery. Suspension.
en tournant,	
Ending with back leg *sur le cou de pied.*	
Arms come to 4th *devant* (arm over supporting leg in first, the other in 2nd.)	Suspension.

3–4: *Pas de bourrée en tournant.*   Suspension. Fall.
  ending in fourth position preparation
5–8: *Pirouettes en dehors,*   Suspension. Potential energy.
  ending in fifth.   Kinetic energy.
Arms rising to 5th in *pirouettes,*   Succession.
  and open to 2nd at the conclusion.
Repeat to other side.

Battement tendus and jetés with pirouettes   2/4

Right leg fifth front. One *battement tendu devant croisé.* One *battement tendu derrière croisé* (with other leg). Four *battements jetés* (with right leg) closing front, back, front, back. Low *développé croisé devant* (left leg) with *relevé* to *demi pointe. Tombé* to fourth position (preparation). *Pirouettes en dedans* ending in *tombé dessus coupé* (back leg on *cou de pied derrière*) and quick *pas de bourrée en tournant en dehors* closing fifth.

Movement	Concept
Preparation: fifth right leg front.	Succession.
Port de bras to 4th *en l'air,* left arm up.	
1–2: One *tendu devant croisé* (right leg).	Opposition.
Arms in 4th *en l'air*	Suspension. Opposition.
3–4: One *tendu derrière croisé* (left leg) Arms remain	Opposition.
5–8: Four *jetés* in *seconde* (right leg) closing front, back, front, back. Arms in 2nd	Kinetic energy. Opposition. Suspension.
1–2: *Petit développé devant croisé* (left leg) with *relevé* to half *pointe.* Arms in 4th *en l'air.*	Kinetic energy. Suspension, Suspension. Opposition.
3–4: *Tombé en avant* to fourth position, preparation.	Fall.
Arms in 4th *devant,* preparation for *pirouettes*	Potential energy.
5–8: *Pirouettes en dedans, Tombé, coupé, pas de bourrée en tournant*	Suspension. Kinetic energy. Fall. Succession. Suspension.
Finishing in fifth.	
Repeat to other side.	

Battements frappés, petits battements sur le cou de pied   2/4 or 6/8
On diagonal from corner # 6 (repeat on the other side from corner # 4).
Four *battements frappés* in *écarté devant*. Four counts of *petits
battements sur le cou de pied*, rising on *demi pointe*. *Demi plié* bringing
working leg to *retiré*, *relevé* in *développé écarté devant*. *Tombé, pas de
bourrée* to fourth position (preparation). *Pirouettes en dehors, fouetté
en dehors* ending on *cou de pied devant*, supporting leg in *demi plié*.
Repeat three times on diagonal to corner, ending with *chaînés*.

Movement	Concept
Preparation: Right leg fifth front. *Dégagé* to *pointe tendue écarté devant*, place working leg on *cou de pied*.	Succession. Opposition.
Arms in 4th *devant*, right arm in front.	
1–4: Four *battements frappés* in *écarté devant*.	Kinetic energy. Rebound.
5–8: Four *counts of petits battements*, rising on *demi pointe*, arms remain.	Suspension.
1–4: *Plié* on supporting leg, *relevé* to *développé, écarté devant*.	Fall. Rebound. Suspension.
Arms in 4th *en l'air*, *Tombé pas de bourrée*.	Fall. Recovery.
to fourth position preparation.	
Arms in 4th *devant*.	Potential energy.
5–6: *Pirouette en dehors*.	Kinetic energy. Suspension.
7–8: *Demi plié* and *fouetté en dehors*. finishing *sur le cou de pied devant* Repeat three times ending with *chaînés* to corner.	Potential energy. Kinetic energy. Suspension.

Ronds de jambe en l'air and renversé   3/4
Right leg in fifth back. One *glissade* (*sans changer*) *double rond de jambe
en dedans* (with back leg) ending with *tombé en avant croisé*. *Coupé
renversé en dehors* ending in *arabesque croisée*. *Pas de bourrée en
tournant* to fourth *position croisée* (preparation). *Fouettés en dedans*
ending with *tombé*, other leg on *cou de pied derrière*. *Coupé dessous,
assemblé dessous* to seconde ending in fifth back.
   Repeat other side.
   Numbers (i.e., 1–4) indicate bars not beats.

Movement	Concept
Preparation: Right leg fifth back.	Succession.
Port de bras to 2nd.	
And 1: *Glissade sans changer,*	Rebound.
back leg opens in extension to	Suspension. Opposition.
seconde, arms through *bras bas* to	
4th *en l'air*, (right arm up).	
And 2: double *rond de jambe en dedans,*	Suspension. Kinetic energy.
wide *tombé en avant croisé.*	Fall.
Arms in complimentary 4th *devant.*	Potential energy.
And 3: *Coupé,*	Potential energy. Rebound.
And 4: *Renversé en dehors,*	Kinetic energy. Suspension.
arms *port de bras* through 5th	
opening to 2nd during *renversé*	
into *arabesque.*	
And 5 and 6: *Pas de bourrée en tournant.*	Suspension. Potential energy.
Arms in 4th *devant.* Potential energy.	
7–8: *Fouettés en dedans,*	Kinetic energy. Suspension.
finishing in *tombé en avant,*	Fall,
to *coupé dessous, assemblé dessous,*	Rebound. Kinetic energy.
(left leg fifth back.)	
Repeat to other side.	

Adagio   3/4

Grand plié in fifth position. Rise to *demi pointe. Développé croisé devant. Tombé* into second *arabesque croisée. Relevé en tournant* (*en dehors*) bringing working leg to *retiré. Développé écarté devant.* Grand *rond de jambe* to *effacé derrière. Tombé en arrière* other leg in *effacé devant. Passé* to second *arabesque croisée. Demi pliés, pas de bourrée en tournant* (*en dehors*) to fourth position *croisée* (preparation). *Pirouettes* in first *arabesque en dedans* ending with *grand fouetté en tournant. Pas de bourrée* to *chassé en avant, pointe tendue croisée derrière,* arms in the *offrande* position (arms in wide 1st position, palms up).

Movement	Concept
Preparation: Right leg fifth front, first	Succession.
port de bras.	
1–4: *Grand plié* in fifth position	Fall. Suspension.
first *port de bras*	Succession.
5–8: Rising on *demi pointe,*	Recovery. Suspension.
port de bras to 5th with the rise	Succession. Suspension.

1–4: *Développé devant croisé,* remaining on *demi pointe.*	Opposition. Suspension.
Arms *port de bras* oppositional to 4th *en l'air.*	Succession. Opposition.
5–6: *Tombé* to second *arabesque croisée, relevé en tournant en dehors* bringing working leg to *retiré.* Arms in 5th.	Fall. Opposition. Rebound. Suspension.
7–8: *Développé* to *écarté devant.* Arms in 4th complimentary *en haut*	Opposition. Suspension.
1–4: *Grand rond de jambe* to *effacé derrière.* Arms extend to high *allongé.*	Opposition. Suspension.
5–6: *Tombé en arrière.* front leg in extension *effacé devant.*	Fall.
Arms in 4th *en haut,*	Opposition. Suspension.
7–8: *Passé* to second *arabesque croisée.*	Recovery. Potential energy.
Arms pass through 1st to *allongé*	Opposition. Suspension.
1–4: *Demi plié,*	Fall.
pas de bourrée en tournant en dehors	Rebound. Suspension.
to fourth position *croisée* preparation.	Fall.
Arms in 4th *devant.*	Potential energy.
5–6: *Pirouettes* in first *arabesque en dedans.*	Rebound. Opposition. Suspension.
And 7: *Grand fouetté en tournant.* Arms, rise through 1st to 5th and end in *allongé* (first *arabesque*).	Fall. Recovery. Suspension.
8: *Pas de bourrée* to fourth position. *Pointe tendue croisée derrière.* Arms in *offrande* position.	Suspension. Opposition.

Allegro

Petit allegro #1   2/4

Sissonne simple devant (to low *retiré*). *Petit jeté élancé en avant croisé. Coupé dessous, assemblé devant croisé. Sissonne simple devant. Petit jeté élancé de côté* ending in *retiré devant. Coupé dessus, assemblé in écarté derrière* closing back. *Sissonne simple derrière. Petit jeté élancé en arrière. Coupé dessus, assemblé derrière. Pas de bourrée en dehors* (toward back leg) *Coupé dessous, assemblé in écarté devant* closing in the back. Repeat on other side.

Note: All the *jetés* in this *enchaînement* are darting, traveling movements ending in low *retiré*. Arms are in *bras bas* for *sissonnes simples* and open to low *devant* (*offrande*) with palms up in *jetés*, and open to *allongé in écarté* for the *assemblés*.

Note: *Pliés* preceding jumps are understood to be potential energy.

Movement	Concept
Preparation: Right leg fifth front, first *port de bras* to 2nd.	
And 1: *Demi plié, sissonne simple devant* ending with front leg in low *retiré.*	Rebound. Fall.
And 2: *Petit jeté en avant croisé,* to low *retiré derrière.*	Rebound. Fall.
And 3: *Coupé dessous.*	Potential energy.
And 4: *Assemblé devant croisé.*	Rebound.
And 1: *Sissonne simple devant.*	Rebound.
And 2: *Petit jeté de côté* to low *retiré devant*	Rebound. Fall.
And 3: *Coupé dessus*	Potential energy.
And 4: *Assemblé* in *écarté derrière* closing back	Rebound.
And 1: *Sissonne simple derrière.*	Rebound.
And 2: *Petit jeté élancé en arrière croisé.*	Rebound. Fall.
And 3: *Coupé dessus.*	Potential energy.
And 4: *Assemblé derrière croisé.*	Rebound.
And 1–2: *Pas de bourrée en tournant en dehors.*	Suspension.
And 3: *Coupé dessous.*	Potential energy.
And 4: *Assemblé* in *écarté devant.* closing fifth back.	Rebound.
Repeat on other side.	

Petit allegro # 2   6/8

A. *Pas de chat. Pas de bourrée en tournant.* Two *sissonnes dessus* (with alternate legs). Repeat A on other side. B. *Sissonne ouverte élancée en avant* ending in second *arabesque croisée. Pas de bourrée en tournant* ending in fourth position *croisée* (preparation). *Pirouettes en attitude en dedans* ending with *soutenu en tournant* (*en dedans*).

Movement	Concept
Preparation: Right leg fifth back.	
And 1: *Pas de chat.*	Rebound.
Arms in oppositional 4th *devant*	
And 2: *Pas de bourrée en tournant*	Suspension.
en dehors.	
3–4: Two *sissonnes dessus* with	Rebound.
alternate legs. As the front leg closes	
the same arm comes to 4th *devant,*	Succession. Suspension.
(complimentary).	
Repeat A on other side.	
And 1–2: *Sissonne ouverte élancée*	Rebound.
en avant. finish in second *arabesque*	Fall.
croisée.	
Arms *allongé devant* (second *arabesque*).	Opposition. Suspension.
And 3–4: *Pas de bourrée en tournant*	
en dehors finish in preparation	Potential energy. Fall.
fourth position *croisée.* Arms in	
4th *devant* (complimentary).	
5–6: *pirouettes en attitude en dedans.*	Rebound. Suspension.
Arms in 4th *en l'air* (oppositional).	Kinetic energy. Suspension.
7–8: *Soutenu en tournant en dedans.*	Suspension. Succession.
Arms through 1st to 5th.	
Repeat other side.	

Grand allegro #1   3/4

On diagonal from upstage corner # 6 (repeat on the other side from corner # 4). Right leg fifth front. *Temps levé tombé. Coupé, ballonné* to *seconde dessous* ending with working leg in *retiré derrière. Temps levé* into second *arabesque croisée* (facing corner # 2). Two steps turning en dehors (upstage) *grand jeté croisé* (*grand jeté en tournant,* Ward Warren 1989, 312) to corner # 8. *Temps levé* in *arabesque.* Two steps turning *en dehors* and *grand jeté croisé* to corner # 2. *Temps levé passé* bringing *arabesque* leg to the front, *tombé. Coupé,* and *chassé* into *chaînés.*

   Note: The last *chaîné* slides directly into the *temps levé tombé.*

   Note: Numbers (i.e., 1–4) indicate bars not beats. The jumps are always on the upbeat.

   Although the *jetés* are treated in this *enchaînement* as rebound they can also be used to illustrate kinetic energy and suspension.

Movement	*Concept*
Preparation: Right leg fifth front.	
And 1: *Temps levé tombé.*	Rebound. Fall.
Arms drop to *bras bas* and open to 2nd.	Potential energy.
And 2: *Coupé derrière.*	Potential energy.
Ballonné to high *seconde* ending with working leg in *retiré derrière.*	Rebound.
Arms in 2nd at height of jump then in 4th complimentary.	Suspension.
And 3: *Temps levé* into second *arabesque croisée.* (toward corner # 2).	Rebound.
Arms *allongé* (second *arabesque*).	Suspension.
And 4: Two steps turning *en dehors. grand jeté croisé.* (toward corner # 8).	Potential energy. Rebound.
Arms *allongé* (second *arabesque*).	Suspension.
And 1: *Temps levé* in *arabesque.*	Rebound.
And 2: Two steps turning *en dehors. grand jeté croisé* (toward corner # 2).	Potential energy. Rebound.
And 3: *Temps levé passé* bringing *arabesque* leg through to *tombé en avant effacé.*	Rebound. Fall.
Arms pass through 1st open to 2nd.	Potential energy. Succession.
And 4: *Coupé, chassé, chaînés.*	Potential energy. Fall. Suspension.

Repeat all the way to downstage corner.

Grand allegro # 2   3/4
Female version:

A. Twice: *Failli* to fourth position *croisée, assemblé volé* in *écarté* position (or *entrechat six volé*, beating front, back, front). B. *Temps levé tombé effacé* (toward corner # 2) *coupé dessous, temps levé* in second *arabesque ouverte* (body turns to face corner # 8). *Pas de bourrée couru* (upstage toward corner # 4) *grand jeté en tournant. Coupé dessous, tombé effacé* (downstage toward corner # 8) *coupé dessous, temps levé* in *second arabesque ouverte* (body turns to face corner # 2). C. *Coupé tombé effacé, pas de bourrée* to fourth position (preparation) *pirouettes en dehors.*

Repeat other side.

Male version:
   Same as above until C: *Coupé, tombé coupé, assemblé devant* to fifth
position, *tours en l'air.*
   Note: Numbers (i.e., 1–4) indicate bars not beats. The jumps are always on the upbeat.

Movement	Concept
Preparation: Right leg fifth front.	
A. 1 and 2: *Failli en avant.*	Rebound. Fall.
assemblé volé in écarté.	Rebound. Suspension.
Arms move through 1st and open to *allongé* in 2nd	
3–4: repeat 1–2	
B. 5 and 6: *Temps levé tombé* in *effacé devant.*	Rebound. Fall.
Coupé dessous, temps levé in second *arabesque*	Potential energy. Rebound.
(turn to face corner # 8)	
Arms move through 1st opening to low 2nd during *coupé,* same	Fall. Succession.
arm as working leg sweeps	Suspension.
through *bras bas* to *allongé devant,* other in arm 2nd. (Position is second *arabesque ouverte* or *épaulée.*)	
7 and 8: *Pas de bourrée couru* (toward corner # 4) *grand jeté en tournant.*	Potential energy. Kinetic energy.
Arms sweep down then through 1st and reach 5th at the height of the jump.	Suspension.
1–2: *Coupé,*	Potential energy.
Repeat 5–8	
C. 3–4: *Coupé*	Potential energy.
temps levé tombé pas de bourrée,	Fall. Suspension.
finishing in fourth position preparation	Fall. Potential energy.
5–8: *Pirouettes en dehors.* finishing in fifth to start to the other side.	Suspension.
Male version :	
C. 3–4: *Coupé, tombé coupé, assemblé devant.*	Potential energy. Suspension. Fall
5–8: *Tours en l'air.*	Rebound. Kinetic energy.

Petite batterie   6/8 or 2/4
On diagonal from corner # 6 (repeat on the other side from corner # 4.)
*Brisé volé en avant, en arrière, en avant. Cabriole devant. Jeté en avant.
Cabriole derrière. Pas de bourrée en tournant en dehors.* One *entrechat
quatre.* Two *piqués en dehors.* Four counts of *chaînés.* Repeat all the way
to the corner.

Movement	Concept
Preparation: right leg in fifth front.	
And 1–2: *Brisé volé en avant:*	Rebound. Suspension.
Arms in 4th *devant,* right arm 1st front, left arm in 2nd, head angled toward front arm.	Succession.
En arrière: Arms to 2nd *allongé* right arm higher than left, head turned to front.	
And 3–4: *Brisé volé en avant, cabriole devant,* arms remain in 4th *devant.*	Rebound.
And 5–6: *Jeté en avant, cabriole derrière.*	Kinetic energy.
Arms 2nd *allongé arabesque croisée*	
And 7–8: *Pas de bourrée en tournant, entrechat quatre.*	Suspension. Rebound.
Arms: *bras bas,* head *épaulée* over front shoulder.	
And 1–4: Two *piqués en dehors* ending with working leg in *retiré,* supporting leg in *demi plié.*	Kinetic energy. Suspension.
And 5–8: *chaînés.*	
Repeat linking to beginning of *enchaînement* without a pause.	Succession.
Repeat on diagonal to downstage corner.	

  Note: The body weight is carried emphatically forward of the line of
gravity in all *brisés volés devant,* with the upper spine arching back in
brisé volé derrière.

Manège (Female)   2/4
From downstage corner # 8, to the right (repeat to the left from corner
2). Four *piqués en dedans. Coupé,* four *emboîtés en tournant.* Two
soutenus en tournant. Travel *en manège* to corner # 6 then on diagonal
to corner # 2, ending with *chaînés* and final pose.

Movement	Concept
Preparation in *pointe tendue devant*, right leg front. Right arm in 1st *devant*, left in 2nd.	Potential energy.
And 1 and 8: Four *piqués en dedans*. impetus forward.	Kinetic energy. Rebound:
And 1–4: Coupé. Four *emboîtés en tournant*.	Rebound: impetus upward
And 5–8: Two *soutenus en tournant*.	Suspension.
Repeat to upstage corner # 6 then on diagonal to corner # 2 ending with *chaînés* into final pose.	Succession.

Manège (Male)   3/4

From downstage corner # 8, to the right (repeat to the left from corner # 2). *Coupé en tournant chassé, coupé en tournant grand jeté* in first *arabesque*. Travel *en manège* to corner # 6. On diagonal toward corner # 2: *coupé, tombé, pas de bourrée, glissade, grand jeté passé derrière* (Ward Warren 1988, 272).

Movement	Concept
Preparation left foot *pointe tendue derrière*.	
And 1 and 2: *Coupé en tournant, chassé.*	Potential energy.
Coupé en tournant, grand jeté	Kinetic energy. Rebound.
Repeat *en manège* to corner # 6.	
1–3: *Coupé, tombé, pas de bourrée, glissade.*	Potential energy
3–4: *Grand jeté passé derrière.*	Kinetic energy.

The class can conclude with series of *fouettés en tournant* (female), and *grandes pirouettes sautillées* (male) and finally, to bring a sense of closure, a sequence of *grands battements* or a *port de bras* and *révérence* for both male and female dancers.

16

CONCLUSION

The evolution of ballet—and, indeed, all forms of dance performance—ultimately depends on its practitioners: dancers, choreographers, and teachers. The dynamics between these three groups are obvious, yet subtle. Dancers apprehend the technique through the body; they integrate and perfect it to become responsive to choreographic demands. Choreographers rely on their knowledge of movement in creating ballets just as they rely on the dancer's proficiency to execute and interpret their work. Teachers reach both into the past and the future. Their experience with their own teachers and the choreographers with whom they worked shaped their development, but their personal understanding of the technique enables them to further the craft as they impart it to their students. This understanding, while based on past experiences, is also informed by current practices.

In a language such as dance, which is passed from master to pupil, the most important aspect of this form of dissemination is the insights teachers bring to it. Dance teachers start life as dancers. Their personal experience initially directs them toward certain conclusions, which, in turn, is influenced by a variety of factors: the particular limitations or givens of their physique, emotional response to movement, the happenstance of studying with this and not that mentor, or working with a specific choreographer within a specific repertoire. These are the subjective factors; by using the personal experience as a springboard, the dancer who becomes a choreographer delves into this knowledge to find his or her own voice. By contrast, the dancer who turns to teaching steps beyond the personal in order to evaluate the technique in a more objective way.

Thus, personal experience needs to refer to the precepts of the technique in order to be applicable to a broad range of student's needs. For example, being short and slightly bow-legged, I turned and jumped with ease. The only means I have for appreciating the struggle of tall, hyperextended students to perform these movements, and help them to cultivate their potential, is through understanding anatomical principles and physical laws, and be able to transmute these principles and laws into the classical gesture.

With all the technical and stylistic options available today, classicism continues to be characterized by certain attributes: adherence to the rules of opposition, the clarity and extension of the line (for example, the extended line of the legs and arms and the exact placement of the torso in relation to the height of the leg in an *arabesque*), the dynamic use of preparatory steps, the cleanliness of execution of each separate step and the delineation between motions (definition of where a step starts and ends). To these technical factors can be added attributes of performance: the ability to let the movement speak—this is usually referred to as expression—and the ability to communicate *joie de vivre* through motion, the sheer pleasure of moving that can be shared kinesthetically by the audience.

The goal of training is to fashion and then gain mastery over the instrument. For the dancer, it is the body/mind that has to be shaped molded and in some cases conquered. And as a dancer's body is used to convey meaning, the shaping and molding of the body/mind needs to be addressed before choreographic or stylistic considerations are relevant. It is rather like a spiritual orientation; the need to believe supersedes the religion one chooses to express that belief.

In this book, I have explored ideas that can further maximize our usage of ballet technique through the use of modern dance concepts. I endeavored to show how these concepts are not only applicable to ballet training, but in fact, are already part of the underpinnings of the classical technique. I do not claim to have exhausted the possibilities, but hope that through a willingness to look beyond the confines of tradition, dancers and teachers will engage in a rediscovery of the dynamics inherent in the craft and thereby appreciate anew the reasons for the tradition.

In this reevaluation, distinguishing between the properties of the technique and the stylistic/choreographic applications becomes paramount. In discussions with colleagues when I queried their use of terminology, sequencing, or emphasis given in specific movements, the answer too often has been, "This is the way I learned it from my teacher." Even to seem to doubt one's mentor appears as a disloyalty, yet we must go further and not shy away from asking hard questions. Conversely, it sometimes takes a long time to fully appreciate the legacy of one's teachers. While studying with Mlle. Lamballe at the Paris Opéra, I chafed under her insistence upon closing with the correct foot in front or back; in my defense I was only twelve at the time. When I made a mistake, she called me stupid and more often than not forced me to sit out the rest of the class. I see this injunction now as a necessary component in integrating a series of movements and acquiring the ability to move with fluidity. On a more positive note, I am still discovering deep truths in the corrections given to me by Cleo Nordi addressing weight transfer and the connections between limbs and torso. And I am old enough to have former students, who are now teachers, telling me that they finally fully appreciate some correction or directive I gave them years ago.

Within that context, I am often disturbed by the loose usage of terminology. Although it is easy to simply hang the name on the movement without considering its meaning, the French terminology is very precise and describes the quality of the movement accurately. A couple of instances come to mind: *coupé, fondu,* and *grand jeté en tournant.*

Coupé is a movement, not a position, it is a transfer of weight from one leg to the other designed to free the supporting leg for motion. It is not synonymous or interchangeable with *retiré,* which describes the action of one leg being "taken away." *Coupé* is often used incorrectly to describe a low *retiré,* instead of calling the position *sur le cou de pied.* Similarly, *fondu* tends to be confused with *plié. Plié* is a bending at the knees on one or two supporting legs. *Fondu,* by contrast, is a composite motion involving the simultaneous straightening of both legs as one extends in the air. Finally, *grand jeté en tournant,* describes sequentially the action of kicking the legs in high extension while performing a turn in the air. *Tour jeté,* although more expedient, inverts the descriptive sequence, and thus does not reflect the action. Admittedly, in a living language new terminology arises when the codified vocabulary is insufficient; however, in that process we need to be vigilant and continue to keep the old nomenclature pure.

Examining long-held beliefs, knowing the potential of the technique in its ability to create an expressive instrument, trusting in the wisdom of its precepts, and separating dogma from fact can lead us on a journey of discovery and wonderful surprises. The goal of the journey is to deepen one's understanding of the body in motion. I offer these pages as the journey's start.

GLOSSARY

FIXED POINTS OF THE STUDIO:

Russian

Front

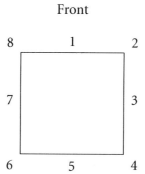

Cecchetti

Front

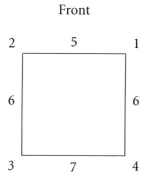

Note: I use the Russian numbering.

Arm positions:

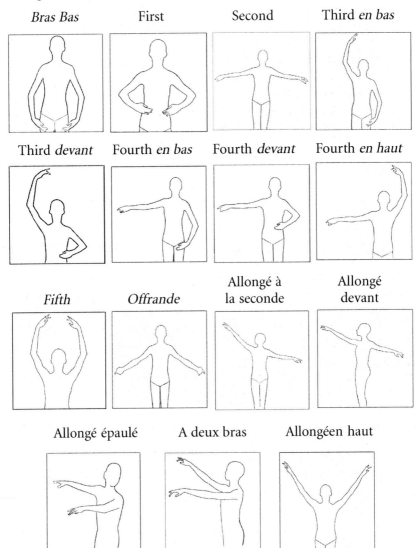

Port de bras
En dehors: 1. From *bras bas,* the arms rise to 1st position, open to 2nd, and return to *bras bas.*
  2. From *bras bas,* the arms rise through 1st position to 5th, open to 2nd, and return to *bras bas.*

En dedans: 1. From *bras bas,* the arms rise directly to 2nd, move to 1st, and return to *bras bas.*
2. From *bras bas,* the arms rise through 2nd to 5th, descend through 1st, and return to *bras bas.*
Note: All schools have specific *port de bras* that are practiced in the center. The above are the basic pathways for the arms from which all others originate.
Complimentary: Same arm as front leg in front (1st) or up (5th); as in *croisé devant épaulé.*
Oppositional: Opposite arm to front leg in front (1st) or up (5th); as in *attitude derrière.*

QUALIFYING TERMS

À demi jambe: As in *retiré à demi jambe.* Fully pointed working foot is lifted to the calf, (midway between knee and ankle) either in front or in the back. *Battement fondu* usually originates in that position.
À la seconde: To the side as in *fondu à la seconde.*
Allongé: Lengthened (literally lying down) refers to arms positions when the hands are placed with palms facing the floor (*arabesques*).
Also position of the body as in *arabesque allongée,* when the leg, body, arms, and head are on the same horizontal plane.
À terre: On the floor, as in *pointe tendue* with toes touching the floor.
Arrondi: Rounded, as in *grand battement arrondi* when from a low *attitude, devant* or *derrière,* the working leg is thrown in a circular path.
Cambré: Bent over, as in *cambré en avant.* A movement curving the spine forward, sideway or backward.
Changé: Changed, as in *sissonne changée* (i.e., front leg opens and closes back, or *glissade changée,* back leg finishes front at the finish).
Sans changer: Without change. Front leg stays in front at completion of movement.
Croisé: Crossed, working leg in an extension crosses the central line of the body. Qualifies front and back positions.
De côté: To the side, also moving sideways, as in *jeté de côté.*
Dégagé: Disengaged, as in *dégagé* to *pointe tendue.*
Derrière: To the back as in *développé derrière.*
Dessous: Under, as in *assemblé dessous.* Working leg starting in fifth front closes in the back.
Dessus: Over, as in *assemblé dessus.* Working leg starting in fifth back closes in front.

Devant: In front as in *battement tendu devant.*

Écarté: Spread wide, qualifies positions to the side. *Écarté devant* is slightly in front of the true second and *écarté derrière* slightly back of that line.

Élancé: Darting, as in *grand jeté élancé.* Cecchetti's sixth basic movement.

En arrière: Moving backward as in *glissade en arrière.*

En avant: Moving forward as in *chassé en avant.*

Enchaînement: : As in a chain, linked. Two or more steps linked together into a phrase. Usually refers to allegro combinations.

En croix: In the shape of a cross. Refers to movements that are done successively front, side, back, and side.

En dedans: Inward, (working leg start in the back and ends in front) as in *pirouette en dedans* (the spin is toward the supporting leg).

En dehors: Outward, as in *rond de jambe par terre en dehors* (working leg starts in front and circles to the back.) Or *pirouette en dehors* (the spin is toward the working leg).

En face: Facing front, the mirror or audience.

Effacé: Erased or shaded, working leg extends in an open direction from the central line of the body. Qualifies front and back positions.

En l'air: In the air. Can refer to a lifted leg as in *développé,* or a jumped step as in *tours en l'air.*

Épaulé: Shouldered, when the front shoulder is emphasized either by bringing the downstage arm forward as in *arabesque épaulée* or by turning the head toward the front shoulder as in 5th position *épaulée.* (Front shoulder corresponds to the front leg in fifth position.)

Épaulement: Shoulderings, describes the position of the body (a spiral of the torso in opposition to the front leg) in relation to the legs as in *croisé, effacé* and *écarté.*

Étendu: Stretched. Cecchetti's second basic movement of dancing.

Fermé: Closed, as in *assemblé fermé* (from a *demi jambe* position as in the end of a *petit jeté,* the working leg stretches downward to fifth during the jump instead of opening into an extension). Or as in *sissonne fermée* when the working leg closes fifth at the conclusion of the jump.

Glissé: Slid or glided: as in *glissade.* Cecchetti's fourth basic movement of dancing.

Ouvert: Open, as in *arabesque ouverte* when the pelvis is open in relation to front, or *sissonne ouverte* when the working leg finishes in an extension off the floor.

Passé: Passed through, when a leg passes from front to back as in *retiré passé* or *grand jeté passé.*

Penché: Tilted, as in *arabesque penchée.*

Plié: Bend, as in *grand plié.* Cecchetti's first basic movement of dancing.

Pointe tendue: Stretched toe retaining contact with floor, as *battement tendu.*

Posé: Placed down as in *posé* to *attitude* (step into *attitude).*

Promenade: Walk about, describes revolving slowly on one leg, also done with partner as in *promenade en attitude.*

Raccourci: Foreshortened, describes the action of an extended leg bending in a percussive motion and ending in a high *retiré* or *demi jambe* position.

Relevé: Raised, as in *battement relevé* (a slow raising of an extended leg). Also a spring onto half or full pointe. Cecchetti's third basic movement of dancing.

Retiré: To take away, as in *retiré passé,* working leg rises to a position with toes touching the supporting leg at the height of the knee (can be in front, side or back). Can also be done to *demi jambe* or *cou de pied* positions.

Sauté: Jumped, as in *retiré sauté.* Cecchetti's fifth basic movement of dancing.

Sautillé: Hopped, as in *pirouettes à la seconde sautillées.* Small hops while revolving in *grandes pirouettes à la seconde* or other big poses.

Sur le cou de pied: as in *petit battement sur le cou de pied.* In front: working foot is wrapped around ankle of supporting leg (foot is slightly flexed and winged). In the back: the heel of working leg touches the back of the supporting leg and is also winged.

Tombé: Fall, as in *temps levé tombé.*

Tourné: Turned, as in *saut de basque en tournant.* Cecchetti's seventh basic movement of dancing.

POSITIONS AND BIG POSES

Arabesque: The working leg is extended behind the body, the supporting leg can be straight, on *demi plié* or on *pointe.* The shoulders and upper torso are square to the line of direction and the pelvis on the working side is slightly rotated outward (Russian School). The arms and orientation of the body determine the naming and numbering of the pose.

First arabesque ouverte: On the right leg, body faces side 3: left leg extended toward side 7, right arm extended toward side 3, left arm extended toward corner 8 (slightly behind the shoulder). The head looks out toward side 3.

First arabesque croisée: On the right leg body faces corner 8: left leg extended toward corner 4, right arm extended toward corner 8, left arm extended toward side 5 or toward corner 4 (advanced). The body spirals to reveal the back to the audience (side 1). The head is angled toward the audience.

Second arabesque ouverte or épaulée: On the right leg body faces side 3: legs in same position as first arabesque but the left arm is extended toward side 3, the right arm extended to side 5, the head angled toward the front (side 1).

Second arabesque croisée: On the right leg body faces corner 8: left leg extended toward corner 4, right arm extended to side 3, left arm extended to corner 8. The head looks out toward corner 8.

Third arabesque ouverte: On the right leg body faces corner 2: left leg extended toward corner 6, both arms extended towards corner 2, right arm higher than left. The head tilts slightly toward right shoulder.

Third arabesque croisée: On the right leg body faces corner 8: left leg extended toward corner 4, both arms extended to corner 8, left arm higher than right. The head tilts slightly toward left shoulder.

Attitude: A pose inspired by the statue of Mercury by Giovanni da Bologna. The working leg is in high extension in the back and bent at the knee to a ninety degree angle or less. Can be done in *croisée* or *effacée* directions. Academic *attitude* requires the knee and the foot to be on the same horizontal plane. Russian *attitude* has less pronounced bent of the knee and allows the foot to be higher than the knee (a more emphatic pose than the academic one.)

Attitude devant: High position in front with working leg bent and lower leg sloping downward. Usually performed in a *croisée* direction.

Positions of the adagio vocabulary: *Devant* and *derrière: en face, effacé, croisé,* and *seconde en face* and *écarté,* in high extensions, are considered big poses. *Grandes pirouettes* can be performed in all these positions.

CONNECTING OR PREPARATORY STEPS

Chassé: Chasing. As used in the *adagio* vocabulary, *en avant:* from fifth position in *demi plié* the front leg slides out with a weight shift onto it, finishing in an extension of the back leg to *pointe tendue derrière.* Can be done in all directions. Also used as a traveling, jumped step, forward, sideways or backward, one leg "chasing" the other.

Coupé: Cut. Usually performed from a *retiré* or *demi jambe* position, supporting leg in *demi plié*. A downward movement designed to free the other leg: substituting one supporting leg for the other. (*Coupé* is a movement, not a position therefore a leg can be *sur le cou de pied* or *à demi jambe* but not in *coupé*.)

Détourné: Turning away. From fifth position on *demi pointe* right leg front: swivel toward back leg changing feet during swivel. Can also be done from a *pointe tendue devant* or *derrière: En dehors:* working leg in *pointe tendue* back: turning toward back leg, ending with same leg in *pointe tendue devant. En dedans:* working leg in *pointe tendue* front: turning toward supporting leg ending with same leg in *pointe tendue derrière.*

Failli: Falling short. E*n avant:* from a fifth position springing up both legs together, back leg opening in the air then sliding through first position to fourth position *devant croisée*, weight centered over front leg (in *demi plié*), back leg is straight and maintains contact with floor. *En arrière:* front leg opening devant then sliding through first position to fourth *derrière effacé* or *croisé* (in *demi plié*), weight centered over back leg, front leg extended usually pointed.

Glissade: Sliding. From fifth position working leg opens to low extension supporting leg pushes off and closes in fifth. Can be done in all directions.

Pas de bourrée: A movement in three steps involving a change of weight with each. The first step brings the leg together, the second steps opens out to a small position either second or fourth, the third step reunites the legs in a closed position. There are many versions; following are the most common.

Pas de bourrée de côté dessous: Fifth position right leg front. The back leg opens to a low *seconde* or draws up into *retiré derrière*, supporting leg in *demi plié*. Step onto left leg in fifth position back on *demi pointe*, step out on *demi pointe* to a small second position with right leg, bring left leg to fifth position front, both legs in *demi plié*.

Pas de bourrée de côté dessus: Fifth position right leg front. The front leg opens to *seconde* or *retiré devant*, steps onto *demi pointe* in fifth position front, left leg steps out to second on *demi pointe*, right leg comes to fifth back, both legs in *demi plié*.

Note: *dessous* and *dessus* can also be done *en tournant*. Also on pointe: *pas de bourrée piqué*, working leg coming to *retiré* with each step.

Pas de bourrée dessus sans changer: As above but from fifth position right leg front, the back left leg opens to the side, steps in fifth front, right leg steps to the side, left closes in fifth back. Also done *en tournant* and often precedes a *fouetté* or a *renversé*.

Pas de bourrée dessous sans changer: As above but front leg open side, steps in fifth back and closes in front. Can also be done in a series of *dessus* and *dessous*, opening in *seconde* between each, as well as *en tournant*.

Pas de bourrée en arrière (usually preceded by a *dégagé devant*): Front leg steps in fifth front, back leg steps out (backward), front leg closes fifth, back leg opens to low *dégagé* back.

Pas de bourrée en avant (usually preceded by a *dégagé derrière*): Back leg steps in fifth back, front leg steps out (forward), back leg closes fifth, front leg opens to low *dégagé* front.

> Note: *En avant* and *en arrière* are usually done in a series, can also be done opening into second position (side to side) or opening to fourth position (forward and backward) either in a *croisé* or an *effacé* direction.

Pas de bourrée couru: A running step comprised of three running steps. Usually precedes a big jump.

Pas de bourrée couru de côté: A run to the side, keeping front leg front, on bend knees, usually followed by a *grand jeté de côté* (Bournonville School). Or on *pointe* in the female vocabulary. In both cases the steps are not limited to three.

Temps levé: Lifting, a jump from one foot to the same foot. As in *petit jeté, temps levé.* Also used with big jump as a link between one step and the next, as in *grand jeté, temps levé* in *arabesque,* or from an *arabesque: temps levé, tombé, fouetté sauté.*

Temps liés: Linking movement. *En avant* from fifth position, the front leg extends to *pointe tendue devant,* other leg in *demi plié,* weight transfers to the front leg through a *demi plié* on both legs and the back one extends to *pointe tendue derrière.* Can be done *en arrière* and *de côté. Temps liés* is also an elementary exercise done as a series *en avant* (forward, side, repeat with other leg) and *en arrière* (backward, side, repeat with other leg). The exercise is also practiced *en l'air* in more advanced classes (Paskevska 1992, 183).

STEPS

Assemblé: To assemble or put together. From a fifth position, *demi plié,* the working leg slides out to a forty-five degree angle off the floor as the supporting leg pushes off the floor. The legs come together in the air just before the dancer lands in fifth position. The movement does not travel and can be done in all directions as well as *dessus* (the working leg opens side from the back and closes in front) and *dessous* (the working leg opens side from the front and closes in the back). Can include beats at intermediate and advanced levels. The legs come together as the jump descends, thus the supporting leg remains perpendicular to the floor. Common mistake: bringing supporting leg toward gesture leg,

    Arms: all *assemblés en face* arms are in held 2nd position. *Assemblé croisé* and *effacé* arms can be in *allongé devant* or à *deux bras.*

Assemblé volé: Flying *assemblé.* Usually preceded by a *failli* or a *pas couru* into an *écarté* position in the air, the working leg opening to a ninety degree angle. This version travels. Can also include beats *entrechat cinq volé* (French School), working leg beating front, back front before landing). Also called *grand assemblé entrechat six volé.*

    Arms: During preparatory step (*failli* or *pas de bourrée*) the arms come to *bras bas,* pass through 1st position and open to *allongé* in 2nd position *écarté* (front arm higher).

Balancé: Rocking (waltz step,) comprised of three steps alternating legs. Can be performed side to side, traveling and *en tournant.* To the right: right leg steps to the side into *demi plié,* left leg comes to *demi jambe* position in the back. Step on *demi pointe* on back leg, front leg slightly lifting off the floor. Come down on right leg in *demi plié.* Repeat to other side.

    Arms: To the right: open arms to 2nd on the first step and bring to 4th position *devant* on second step (left arm front). hold arms until the *balancé* repeats to other side.

Ballonné: Bounced like a ball. Usually preceded by a *coupé,* the gesture legs open into an extension while the supporting leg pushes off. At the height of the jump both legs are straight then the gesture leg does a strong *raccourci* ending à *demi jambe* or *cou de pied* position. Can be done *dessous, dessus* with extension to the side (does not travel), and *en avant* and *en arrière* in *croisé* or *effacé* directions (travels forward or backward.)

    Arms: *dessus* and *dessous:* the arms are in 2nd position during jump and in 4th *devant* upon landing, arm in front same as landing leg (right leg landing, right arm in front.) *En avant* and *en arrière* follows rules of opposition: right leg in front, left arm in front or in 5th.

Ballotté: Tossed like a boat on the waves. A jump from one foot to the other opening the alternating gesture leg *devant* then *derrière.* Russian version: the legs are straight, held together in the air and open to low extension front and back upon landing. Italian version:

the legs pass through a *retiré* position on the way out (*développé*) and the way in (*raccourci* or *enveloppé*). The movement is usually done in an *effacé* direction. The body emphasizes the front extension by arching back and the back position by leaning forward as if rocked. *Ballottés* are a good example of the use of counterbalance.
Arms: to the right, *ballotté devant*: arms in 4th position *devant*, left arm front (opposite to front leg). Head angled emphatically to front shoulder. *Ballotté derrière*: 4th position right arm *devant* (same arm as supporting/landing leg). Head looking over front arm.

Brisé: Broken, shattered. A low, traveled and beaten step resembling an *assemblé* in an *effacé* direction. *En avant*: from a fifth position the back leg opens to *effacé devant*, the supporting leg pushes off and beats behind then in front of the gesture leg, finishing in fifth front. The body is held emphatically forward. *En arrière*: from a fifth position the front leg opens to *effacé derrière*, the supporting leg pushes off and beats in front then back of the gesture leg and finishes in fifth back. The body arches back during the jump. Often done in a series in the same direction.
Arms: to the right *en avant* (right leg in fifth back): arms are held in 4th position *devant*, right arm front. Head is angled over front arm. *En arrière* (right leg in fifth back): 4th position *devant*, left arm in front. Head angled emphatically to front shoulder.

Brisé volé: Flying *brisé*. From fifth position the movement begins as a *brisé en avant* with gesture leg opening to *effacé devant*, the back leg beats back-front and finishes in a low extension *devant croisé*, the front leg describes a low *rond de jambe en dehors* then beats back-front (becoming the supporting leg) the other leg is extended *derrière* then it describes a low *rond de jambe en dedans*, beats front back finishing with other leg in *croisé devant*. The body emphatically leans forward when leg is in front and arches back with the *derrière* extension. Can be done with low jumps as well as very high ones the body and legs creating a C (everted when working leg is in the back) in the air.
Arms: to the right *devant*: arms are in 2nd *allongé*, right arm lower than left, head turned in the same direction as arm, body leaning forward. *Derrière*: right arm rises to high *allongé* 2nd, left arm lower, the head turns toward left arm and body arches back.

Cabriole: Caper, like a goat. Usually preceded by a *glissade* or *failli*, the gesture leg opens in an extension and the supporting leg beats underneath propelling the gesture leg higher before landing either in fifth position *(cabriole fermée)* or into a *tombé*. It can also finish on one leg the working leg held in an extension *(cabriole ouverte)*. Can be performed front, side or back. It can also include a double beat.

> Arms: *cabriole devant*: opposite arm to front leg rises through 1st position to 4th position *en haut*. *Cabriole de côté*: arms remain in 2nd. *Cabriole derrière croisée*: arms are in 2nd *arabesque croisée* position (*allongé devant*) opposite arm to front leg in front. *Cabriole derrière ouverte*: arms are in first *arabesque* position, same arm as front leg in *allongé devant*.

Chaîné: (also called *déboulé* by French School): Linked like a chain. A series of turns with feet either in fifth or first position traveling in any direction. The weight shifts rapidly from one foot to the other with each half turn, the head spotting in the direction of travel.

> Arms: to the right, from a preparation in *pointe tendue devant croisée*, arms in 4th *devant* position, the front arm opens with first step then both arms are held in 1st position. They can also open slightly with each turn.

Changement de pied: Changing of the feet. A straight up and down jump from fifth to fifth changing feet in the air.

> Arms: usually held in *bras bas* position.

Chassé: Chasing. In adagio vocabulary the step begins in fifth, *en avant*: front leg slides out into a fourth position and back leg extend to *pointe tendue derrière*. *En arrière*: back leg slides out through fourth and front leg extends in *pointe tendue devant*. Can also be done to the side.

> Arms: Usually arms sweep through 1st position to 4th *en haut*, opposite arm to the front leg is up. But can also go directly to ending position as in *chassé* to *arabesque*.

Chassé sauté: Chasing. Usually done in a series one foot chasing the other. Can be performed in all direction and *en tournant*. *En avant*: right foot fifth position front: front foot slides forward into fourth position, with a small spring off the floor the feet come together in the air. The landing occurs with feet still in fifth but the front foot slides rapidly into a fourth position and the movement is repeated in a series.

> Arms: usually arms are in 4th position *en haut*, opposite arm to front leg is up.

Emboîté: Fitting in (put into a box). A light springing step from one foot to the other. Can be done into *demi jambe* position, low *attitude devant* position, or low *arabesque*.

Arms: *devant*: arms are held in 4th position *en haut. Derrière*: arms
are in 2nd *allongé*, upstage arm slightly higher.

Emboîté en tournant: turning *emboîté* is done with a half turn usually
on a diagonal to a *demi jambe* position alternating gesture foot in
front of supporting leg. The same arm as working leg is placed in
front (4th position *devant*).

Arms: to the right, preparatory position in fifth right foot front,
arms in 4th *devant* (right arm front). With the first jump as
the back leg (left) rises to *demi jambe* position front, the arms
come into 4th position *devant* left arm front. With the next
jump the right arm comes front. This exchange is repeated
with each jump and half turn. The head is always angled toward the front arm and spots in the direction of travel.

Entrechat: Cross caper. A straight up and down jump. The legs cross
rapidly in the air bypassing each other beginning and ending in
fifth position. *Entrechat quatre*: front foot beats back ends in front.
Entrechat six: front leg beats back, front ends in the back. *Entrechat
huit:* front leg beats back, front, back ends in the front. *Royale*: front
foot beats front ends in the back. Odd numbered *entrechats* end
on one foot: *entrechat trois*: front foot beats in front, ends in low
retiré position in the back (can be reversed ending in front).
Entrechat cinq: front leg beats back ends in low *retiré* position in
front (can be reversed to end in the back).

Arms: with all even numbered *entrechats* the arms are held in *bras
bas*. With *entrechat six* and *huit* done in a series the arms can
be held in 2nd *allongé* to facilitate the jump. With all odd
numbered *entrechats* when the landing is on one foot the same
arm as the landing leg is brought forward, 4th position *devant*.

Fouetté: Whipped. A whipping motion of one leg accompanied by a
half or full turn.

Fouetté en dehors: usually preceded by a *pas de bourrée en tournant* as
preparation or a *pirouette en dehors* to the right: the right leg extends front at 90 degrees, (supporting leg in *demi plié*), whips to
the side (supporting leg still in *demi plié*) and with a *relevé* on
pointe the gesture leg comes to *retiré* (touches back of the knee
and ends in front) as the body revolves (*pirouette*). Can conclude
in fourth or fifth position or in a big pose like *attitude derrière*. (In
adagio or at the barre starts with a *retiré* and *développé* to front
followed by the "whip" to the side and *pirouette*.)

Arms: to the right: during the *pas de bourrée en tournant* the arms
pass through 1st position and come to 4th position *devant*
(right arm front). The front arm open to 2nd position as the

gesture leg whips from front to side, arms then come to 1st position during the turn.

Fouetté rond de jambe en tournant: as above but done in a series as in thirty-two *fouettés* in Swan Lake. The gesture leg extends to *devant*, supporting leg on *demi plié* between each turn.

> Arms: as above, the arms open to 2nd between each turn (when the leg opens devant).

Fouetté en dedans (pirouette en dedans): from a fourth position, the back leg extends to second at ninety degrees then comes to *retiré* in front of the knee as the body revolves. Concludes in fifth or fourth position front. (As above, can also be done at the barre or in adagio from an extension in the back).

> *Note:* when done in a series the foot touches front of the knee then back and the leg extends directly to second between turns.

> Arms: to the right: in the preparation the arms are in 4th *devant*, right arm front (complimentary, same as supporting front leg). As the back leg extends to side front arm opens to 2nd position then both arms rise directly to 5th.

> Note: the left arm does not pass through 1st position. At the conclusion of the *fouetté* the arms open directly to 2nd position or *offrande* position.

Grand fouetté en tournant: This *fouetté* refers to the body "whipping" away from extended leg in *en dedans* action and toward extended leg in *en dehors* action. *En dehors:* from an extension to the front at ninety degrees, *relevé-plié* as preparation then the gesture leg sweeps through first position to *derrière*. The body turns towards the leg to finish in a *devant en l'air* extension.

> Arms: right leg in extension *devant:* arms are in 4th position *en haut* (left arm up), as the gesture leg sweeps through the left arm moves through 1st position to 2nd position (*port de bras en dedans*) and rises again to 5h (4th position *en haut*), the right arm remains in 2nd position.

Grand fouetté en dedans: From an *arabesque, relevé-plié* as preparation, the gesture leg sweeps through first position to ninety degrees *devant.* The body turns away from the working leg to finish in *arabesque.*

> Arms: to the right, left leg in *arabesque:* arms come to 2nd position during *relevé-plié* and sweep through 1st position to 5th (held in 5th during turn) then open to *arabesque* position or open to 2nd (in anticipation of the *relevé-plié*) if the movement is to be repeated.

Note: *Grand fouetté en dehors* and *en dedans* are performed either on half or full *pointe* or as a jump. It can also be done with either a half turn or a full revolution. With a full turn, the gesture leg is held in position after the swing until the turn has been completed. (*en dehors*: the leg is held in *arabesque*. *En dedans*: the leg is held in front.)

Note: The term *fouetté* can refer to any action that involves the body turning either away or toward an extended leg (in contrast to a *grand rond de jambe* where the leg circles from one position to the next and the body maintains its direction). It is used in adagio sequences as in *développé* to *écarté* and *fouetté* to *effacé devant* (body turning toward extended leg which ends in the *devant* position.)

Gargouillade: Gurgling or gargling. Usually preceded by a *coupé* this step is like a *pas de chat* with *ronds de jambe en l'air*. From fifth position right leg front: back leg *coupé*, right leg rises *en l'air* as in *pas de chat* and executes a *double rond de jambe en dehors* as the push off occurs. The left leg pushes off and executes a *double rond de jambe en dedans* and stretches out as the landing occurs to close in fifth position front.

> Arms: during *coupé* the arms are in 4th position *devant* (same arm front as supporting leg). They open to 2nd position during the jump and finish in 4th *devant* (same arm front as front leg).

Jeté: Thrown. A jump from one foot to the other. There are several versions of this step.

Petit jeté dessus: from a fifth position right leg front: the back leg (left) opens to a low *en l'air* position as the right leg pushes off the floor. The landing occurs on the left leg the right leg in low *retiré derrière*.

> Arms: during jump arms are held in 2nd position and come to 4th position *devant* with the landing (the same arm as the landing leg is in front.)

Petit jeté dessous: the front leg (right) opens as the back leg pushes off. The landing occurs on the right leg with the left in low *retiré devant* position.

> Arms: as above, landing with arms in 4th *devant* (same arm as landing leg in front)

> *Note*: both *jetés* can include a beat.

Petit jeté élancé: this movement is the same as *dessus* or *dessous* but travels forward, side or back.

Grand jeté en avant: big throw. Usually preceded by a preparatory step like *pas de bourrée couru* or *glissade* which is followed by a *grand* *battement devant* while the back leg pushes off the floor. At the apex of the jump the legs are stretched and lifted to a split, one leg in extension *devant* the other *derrière*. The landing occurs on the front leg the other in *arabesque*.

> Arms: the position of the arms varies with the placement or direction of the *jeté*. *Croisé*: the opposite arm to the front leg is *allongé devant*. Can also be done with arms in *offrande* position (Bournonville *jeté*). *Ouvert- épaulé*: opposite arm to front leg is in *allongé devant*. *Ouvert* can also be done into first *arabesque* position (same arm as front leg in *allongé devant*).

> Note: the arms from a 2nd position always sweep through *bras bas* and pass through 1st position during the preparatory step.

Grand jeté en arrière: the movement begins with a *grand battement derrière* as the supporting leg pushes off and rises to a *devant* position. The landing occurs on the back le.g., the front leg in a *devant* extension.

> Arms: from 2nd position arms sweep through *bras bas* and open in *offrande* position.

Grand jeté de côté: often preceded by a *pas de bourrée couru de côté* (the front leg stays in front) then a *grand battement* to the side the other leg pushes off the floor and rises to a high *seconde*. The landing occurs on the first leg then the second leg closes in fifth front.

> Arms: arms open to 2nd position with the jump.

Grand jeté passé: as *grand jeté en avant* but at the height of the jump the front leg comes through *retiré* to *développé derrière*, (if the *jeté* is initiated by the right leg the landing occurs on the left leg). The movement can also omit the *passé*: straight legs passing each other in the air.

> Arms: the position of the arms during jump can be either in *allongé devant* (opposite arm to front leg) or in 2nd or 5th position *allongée*.

> Note: *grand jeté passé* can also be done to the side (second leg passing through to *arabesque*). (Ward Warren 1989, 273)

Grand jeté en tournant: usually done either from a downstage corner on a diagonal or from the side traveling across the studio. From downstage corner 2, preparation in *pointe tendue derrière croisée*, right foot back. *Pas couru:* step on back leg still facing corner 2, two more steps turning the body to upstage corner 6, left leg kicks in a *grand battement* still facing corner 6, immediately the other leg pushes off the floor in a *grand battement derrière* as the body turns in the air to face corner 2 and the legs bypass each other in the air. The landing is on the left leg the right in *arabesque croisée*.

(It can also be done into open position, starting with left leg in *pointe tendue derrière, épaulée,* finishing in an *arabesque ouverte.*)

Arms: during preparatory step arms are in 2nd position then sweep through *bras bas* and 1st , and rise to 5th with the push off the floor. They can be held in 5th through the landing or open into an *allongé* position.

Note: I believe that it is Luigi Albertieri (1860–1930, studied with Cecchetti and opened a school in New York in 1915) who first used "*tour jeté*" instead of *grand jeté en tournant.* Possibly because *tour jeté* is more expedient, however *tour jeté* does not describe the action accurately.

Grand jeté en tournant entrelacé: same as above but at the height of the jump the legs beat as they bypass each other.

Arms: as above

Pas de basque (originally called *pas de Russe*)**:** A movement in three counts. There are several versions.

Pas de basque en avant: From fifth position right leg front, right leg extends to *pointe tendue devant croisée,* left leg on *demi plié,* gesture leg does a *rond de jambe par terre en dehors* to *seconde,* left leg remaining in *demi plié.* Left leg pushes off to transfer weight onto right, the right leg is now in *demi plié.* The left leg slides (*chassé*) through first position to fourth *devant* with transfer of weight onto it, the right leg extends in *pointe tendue derrière croisée.*

Arms: Beginning in 2nd position the arms come through *bras bas* to 1st position, open to 2nd with *demi rond de jambe* to side, sweep through *bas bas* and 1st during the *chassé* and rise to 4th position *en haut* (opposite arm to front leg is up). They can also open to the *offrande* position.

Pas de basque en arrière: As above with the back leg extending to *pointe tendue croisée derrière, rond de jambe en dedans* to *seconde,* transfer of weight onto extended leg and sliding through first position to fourth *derrière croisée,* front leg in *pointe tendue devant croisée.*

Arms: As above. The *port de bras en dehors* can also reverse with arms ending in 2nd position.

Petit pas de basque: the extension to front or back is omitted and the working leg extends directly to *seconde,* ending the movement as above either *en avant* ending with *pointe tendue croisée derrière* or *en arrière* with *pointe tendue croisée devant.*

Arms: arms begin in 2nd position, and sweep through *bras bas* and 1st during transfer of weight and open to *offrande* position.

Petit pas de basque piqué: As above the gesture leg opens directly to *seconde*, other leg in *demi plié* pushes off and comes to *retiré* position then drops to fourth position front. This movement often serves as preparation for *pirouettes en dehors*.

Petit pas de basque sauté: as above but adding a little jump to the transfer from *seconde* to *seconde*. Can also be done *en tournant:* preceded by a step or a *chassé*, to the right: step on right leg, kick left leg into low *seconde* as the push off begins with a half turn in the air, finishing the turn by bringing right leg to *demi jambe devant* position.

> Arms: without turning the arms are same as above. With turn the arms are held in 2nd position at the apex of the jump and come to 1st position as the body turns and lands.

Grand saut de basque en tournant: usually preceded by a *chassé sauté*. To the right: the left leg kicks in *grand battement devant* as the right pushes off the floor and comes to a *retiré* position during the turn in the air. The landing is on left leg the right leg in *retiré*. Can be done in a series.

> Arms: the arms are in 2nd position during the preparatory step then sweep through *bras bas* and 1st position (during the initial *battement)* and are held in 5th during the turn in the air and through the landing, opening to 2nd position with the next preparation.

Pas de chat: Step of the cat. To the right: right leg fifth position back: the right leg is lifted to high *retiré* (not touching the supporting knee) as the left leg pushes off the floor and is lifted to a high *retiré*. The landing occurs on right leg with left leg closing in fifth *devant*. Can be done in a series to the same side. (Preobrajenskaya taught *pas de chat* thus: from fifth position right leg back, back leg opens to straight extension in *effacé* as the left leg pushes off into *retiré*. The landing is on the right leg, the left leg closing immediately after.)

> Arms: held in 4th *devant* (same arm front as back leg) with the body leaning forward toward direction of travel, head angled over front arm.

Pas de cheval: Horse's step. The right foot extends in *pointe tendue devant*, with a little hop on supporting leg the right leg bends and stretches (as if pawing the ground), weight is transferred to right leg while the left does a little *développé* and paws the ground (the transfer of weight from one leg to the other occurs during the hop.) Can be done in a series.

Arms: arms are held in low 2nd position with head turning toward each alternating front leg. A *port de bras en dehors* can also be done.

Pas de ciseaux: Scissors step. Usually preceded by a *pas de bourrée couru,* or *tombé* into fourth or a *failli.* To the right: right leg kicks in a *grand battement devant* as the left leg pushes off and then rises to *grand battement devant.* The legs pass each other in the air in front, the landing occurs on the right leg while the left leg drops into fourth position *devant (plié* on the front leg).

Arms: during the preparation the arms sweep from 2nd position through *bras bas* and 1st rising to 5th with the jump and opening out into a wide 5th with the landing. The head is turned up toward the front arm.

Pas de papillon: Butterfly step. Usually preceded by a *tombé* into fourth position, weight on the front leg: back leg kicks back followed quickly by the second leg kicking back, both with slightly bent knees. Ending with second leg sliding through first position into *tombé en avant* (fourth position). Often done in a series of light springy jumps.

Arms: with *tombé* the body leans over the front leg with arms in a loose *bras bas* position then they describe a semi circle passing through 5th position both arms moving in the same direction.

Pied à la main: A stretching movement performed to loosen hip joint muscles. Usually done at the barre after the *petit battement sur le cou de pied* exercise. Holding the heel of the working leg in the hand (*demi plié* on supporting leg) stretching the leg forward then to the side (supporting leg straightens), keeping the body vertical.

Pirouette: Turn or spin. Can be done in a variety of poses and positions, in *retiré,* and in *arabesque, attitude, à la seconde, en dehors* and *en dedans.* (For a detailed discussion of *pirouettes* see Paskevska, 1992.)

Pirouette en dehors: To the right from fifth position *demi plié* on both legs, right leg front: the front foot pushes off and rises to *retiré* (in front of the supporting knee) while the left foot pushes off into a *relevé* on *demi pointe* or *pointe.* The spin is toward the working leg. Ending in fifth or fourth position back. From fourth position to the right: the left leg is in *demi plié,* the right is straight (weight on the front leg, When done on *pointe* or partnered the fourth position is narrower and both knees can be bent). The *relevé* is on the left (front) leg the right leg placed in *retiré* during the turn (front of the knee). Ending in fourth or fifth position back.

Arms: preparation: For *pirouettes* from fifth position, arms are in 4th *devant,* same arm in front as front leg. For *pirouettes* from fourth position opposite arm to front leg in front. The front arm opens slightly to side with push off the floor, then both arms are held in 1st position during *pirouette.* (The action of the arm opening to the side engages the torso therefore the force of that opening must be commensurate with the number of turns intended, i.e., for one *pirouette* little force beyond the torque created by the feet is needed, for two or more *pirouettes* more force is required so the gesture must be more emphatic.)

Pirouette en dedans: From fifth position right leg front (to the right), *demi plié* on both legs. Left leg pushes off and rises to *retiré* (front of the knee) while right leg pushes off into *relevé.* The turn is toward the supporting leg. Ending in fourth or fifth position left leg front. From fourth position: right leg in *demi plié,* left leg straight in back. Left leg pushes off and rises to *retiré* (front of the supporting knee) while the right pushes off into *relevé.* Ending in fourth or fifth in front. (The working leg can also open to *second* position before coming to *retiré* in which case the fourth position preparation is wider than for *pirouettes en dehors* and the movement is called a *fouetté en dedans.*)

Arms: preparation: For *pirouettes* from fifth position arms are in 4th *devant,* same arm as front leg in front. The front arm opens to 2nd position as working leg comes to *retiré* then both arms in 1st position during turn. For *fouetté en dedans* from fourth position: arms in 4th position *devant,* same arm as front leg in front. As the working leg opens to *seconde* the front arm open to 2nd position, then both arms rise to 5th and open directly to 2nd or *offrande* position at the end of the turn.

Grandes Pirouettes: Big spins. Can be done in all big poses *en dehors* and *en dedans.*

A la seconde is usually executed from a second position preparation, all others usually start from a fourth position preparation.

Note: The fourth position preparation is wider for *grandes pirouettes* than for those in *retiré,* this creates more force as well as placing the body in an optimum position to cope with the weight displacement necessitated by the gesture leg being further away from the axis.

Renversé: turned upside down. Usually preceded by a *tombé* into deep fourth position. *En dehors: coupé* with back leg, the front leg pushes off into *grand battement devant* to *grand rond de jambe en dehors,* the supporting leg in *relevé,* ending in either an *arabesque croisée* or *attitude* with strongly arched spine, followed quickly by a *pas de bourrée en dehors en tournant. En dedans:* from a high extension *a la seconde* or a first *arabesque croisée,* the working leg comes to a high *retiré* (front of the supporting knee) the supporting leg in *demi plié,* the body tilted sideways toward gesture leg. The body rotates in that position until it comes facing front again then gesture leg opens to high *seconde* position, supporting leg in *relevé,* the body leaning emphatically away from extended leg.

Arms: *En dehors,* for *renversé* into *arabesque:* arms in 1st position during *tombé* rising to 5th during *grand rond de jambe* and opening to 2nd (palms up) when *arabesque* is reached. For *renversé* into *attitude:* arms in 1st position during *tombé,* opening to 2nd with the beginning of *grand rond de jambe,* then into 4th *en haut (port de bras en dedans),* same arm up as *attitude* leg. *En dedans:* arms come to 1st position with *retiré* and open to a wide *offrande* position with the high *seconde.*

Sissonne: Derived from *ciseaux* (scissors) or possibly named after a teacher of the 19th century Mons. Sissonne. There is a great variety of *sissonnes,* the step starts from both feet, the legs open in the air and the landing occurs on one leg (*sissonne ouverte*) or closes quickly after the landing in fifth (*sissonne fermée*).

Sissonne simple devant: From fifth position springing up from both legs the front leg coming to low *retiré devant* as the landing occurs on back leg. Can also be done with a beat in which case it duplicates *entrechat trois* or *cinq.*

Arms: Can be held in *bras bas* or rise to 4th position *devant* same arm front as landing leg.

Sissonne simple derrière: As above, but with back leg coming to low *retiré.* Can also be done with a beat.

Arms: As above.

Sissonne fermée: En avant: from fifth position springing up from both legs, back leg opens to *arabesque* in the air. Landing on front leg, back leg closing quickly in fifth. *En arrière:* the front leg open *devant,* landing on back leg, front leg closing quickly in front. *De côté* can be done *dessus* or *dessous.*

Arms: *En avant:* arms in *allongé devant* (second *arabesque* position) opposite arm to front leg in front. *En arrière:* arms in

4th *en haut* opposite arm to front leg is up. *De côté dessus* and *dessous*: arms in 2nd position during jump coming to 4th *devant* as the landing occurs, same arm in front as front leg. (When done very rapidly arms can remain in 2nd position with the head acknowledging the landing by turning toward the front leg).

Sissonne changée fermée en avant: The front leg opens into *arabesque*.
  Arms: Can be done with first *arabesque (ouverte* and *croisée*) or second *arabesque* arm positions.

Sissonne changée fermée en arrière: The back leg opens to *devant* position.
  Arms: In 4th position *en haut*, opposite arm to front leg is up.

Sissonne ouverte en avant: The gesture leg remains in *arabesque* after the landing.
  Arms: As in *sissonne fermée en avant*.

Sissonne ouverte en arrière: The front leg remains in *en l'air devant* position after landing.
  Arms: as in *sissonne fermée en arrière*.

Sissonne ouverte de côté: the gesture leg remains in *à la seconde* position after the landing. Usually followed by a *coupé* and *assemblé*. Can also be done with a *developpé* into the open position.
  Arms: in 4th position *en haut*, same arm as gesture leg is up, the body leaning emphatically away from gesture leg in the landing the head turned toward the 2nd position arm and angles toward the floor.

Note: *Sissonnes ouvertes* can also change feet and be done with a *développé* into the open position. Also *sissonnes changée* can be done *en tournant: en dehors*, after push off rotate in the air toward back leg, which then opens *devant en l'air*. *En dedans*: after push off rotate in the air toward back leg, front leg opening to *arabesque*.

Soubresaut: Sudden jump. A simple jump from fifth to fifth keeping legs together (front foot remains front.) Can also be done traveling forward, backward, or to the side.
  Arms: when in place: arms in *bras bas*. Traveling forward in *croisé* direction: both arms in *allongé devant* with upstage arm higher, head straight looking toward arms or angled to the front. Traveling backward in *croisé* direction: arms in low 2nd position *allongé* and slightly behind the body. Traveling sideways (toward front foot): as in traveling forward but arms slightly more to the side with head turned in the direction of travel.

Sous-sus: Under-over. A *relevé* on both legs in fifth position to *demi* or full *pointe* (front foot remains front.)

Arms: can be held in *bras bas* or rise to 5th position.

Soutenu dessous: Sustained. From fifth position, right leg in front: front leg opens to side *pointe tendue*, supporting leg in *demi plié*. As the supporting leg pushes off into *relevé* the gesture leg returns quickly to fifth back, the weight is on both feet.

Arms: from 2nd position arms sweep through *bras bas* to 5th position.

Soutenu dessus: As above, but the back leg open to side and ends in fifth front.

Arms: As above.

Note: Movement can be done opening gesture leg to front (*devant*) or opening back leg back (*derrière*).

Soutenu en tournant en dehors: From fifth position right leg front: front leg opens side, legs come together in *relevé*, right leg back, weight is on both feet while body rotates toward back leg, back leg switches with front leg during the swivel. Ending with right leg in front on *demi* or full *pointe* body facing front *épaulé*.

Arms: As *soutenu* without turning.

Soutenu en tournant en dedans: As above, but the back leg opens to side, comes in front *sous-sus*, then switches to back during the swivel.

Arms: As above.

Note: both *soutenus en tournant* can be done with a *piqué* to *demi* or full *pointe* followed by the rotation.

Temps de cuisses: Thigh movement. A compound step comprised of a low *retiré passé* to fifth position and a quick *sissonne*. *Dessus:* from fifth position right foot front: left leg comes to a low *retiré passé*, closing in fifth front, followed by a *sissonne de côté* keeping left leg in front. *Dessous:* from fifth position right leg front, the right leg executes the *retiré passé* closing in the back followed by a quick *sissonne de côté* keeping right leg in the back.

Arms: *dessus:* from a 2nd position arms come to 4th *devant* same arm forward as gesture leg and remain there through the *sissonne*. Body leans forward toward gesture leg and head is angled over front arm. *Dessous:* as above but the same arm as ending front leg is in front.

Temps de flèche: Arrow step. Usually preceded by a *pas couru, glissade* or *failli*. To the right, the right leg rises in *grand battement devant* as the left leg pushes off the floor. In the air the left leg comes through a high *retiré passé* to *devant en l'air* (like shooting an arrow through a bow.) Landing is on right leg, the left remains in extension.

Arms: during preparation arms are in 2nd position then sweep through *bras bas* to 5th or 4th *en haut*, opposite arm to front leg up.

Temps de poisson: Fish's step. This is similar to *failli* but the legs are held together at the apex of the jump, body in *effacé*, with an emphatic arching of the back. Back leg opens in *arabesque* on the descent, the landing is on front leg the back leg swinging through first position to *tombé en avant* (fourth position weight on front leg).

Arms: from 2nd position arms sweep though *bras bas* to 5th, back is highly arched, and open to 2nd palms up.

Tours de reins: Kidney jump (the reference to the kidneys acknowledges the highly arched back during the leap). Usually done in a series linked by a *coupé* or *chassé coupé*, on a diagonal or *en manège*. *Grand jeté* is performed *en tournant* with a highly arched back at the apex of the jump. The back leg can be either in *arabesque* or *attitude.*

Arms: usually performed with 4th *en haut* position arms (oppositional, same arm up as back leg) at the apex of the jump.

Tours en l'air: Turns in the air. From fifth position right leg front, springing up and turning in the air one or more times. The front foot changes to fifth back at the beginning of the turn. Landing with right foot in the back. *Tours en l'air* can end in a variety of poses on one leg or on one knee.

Arms: preparation: arms in 4th *devant* opening slightly to 2nd during take off and coming to 1st during the turn. With the landing arms open to 2nd or *offrande* position.

NOTES

Chapter 1

1. Release technique has applicability to all types of dance by teaching students to let go of habitual patterns and through imagery to access the deepest layers of the body. (See Skinnerreleasingtechnique.com or Klientechnique.com)
2. For the sake of clarity, "motion" is used in a generic sense, while "movement" refers to the codified steps of the technique.

Chapter 2

1. Camargo (1710–1770) shortened her skirt to reveal her mastery of the *petit allegro* vocabulary.
2. Ironically, it is modern dancer Doris Humphrey in her *The Art of Making Dances* who explained how to use stage space to maximize the desired effect of choreographic patterns. Her views support entirely the structures used by Petipa.
3. Appeared in the libretto for Daphnis and Chloe and later reprinted in the *London Times*.
4. Agrippina Vaganova (1879–1951) developed a syllabus after the Revolution in Russia that was adopted by Eastern bloc countries as well as many schools throughout the world.

Chapter 7

1. It is true that today ballet choreographers borrow many elements from the modern dance aesthetic and deformalize certain motions to suit their need.

Chapter 8

1. This usage also applies to all *grandes pirouettes*; see Paskevska 1992.
2. The Vaganova *chassé* opens the front leg without passing through fifth position. However, it must be noted that this style encourages an emphatic verticality in response to performing and training on a raked stage (Ward Warren 1989, 232).

Chapter 9

1. Some dancers today seem unaware of the quality they project through their glance and appear to challenge the audience in some unspecified contest; I personally find this very disconcerting.

Chapter 10

1. Defined by Laban, The kinesphere refers to the reach space around the body in all directions, creating a three-dimensional sphere of motion (Bartenieff 1980, 25).

BIBLIOGRAPHY

Anderson, Jack. *Ballet and Modern Dance, A Concise History*. Princeton, NJ: Princeton Book Publisher, 1992.

Anderson, Brenda, J., Adriana A. Alcantara, and William T. Greenough. "Motor Skill Learning: Changes in Synaptic Organization of the Rat Cerebellar Cortex." *Neurobiology of Learning*, 66(2, Sept.) (1996).

Bainbridge Cohen, Bonnie. *Sensing, Feeling and Action*. Northampton, MA: Contact Editions, 1993

Banes, Sally. *Terpsichore in Sneakers*. Boston: Houghton Mifflin Company, 1977.

Barringer, Janice, and Sarah Schlesinger. *The Pointe Book*. Princeton, NJ: Princeton Book Publishers, 1990.

Bartenieff, Irmgard, and Dori Lewis. *Body Movement*. New York: Gordon and Breach Science Publishers., 1980.

Beaumont, Cyril, and Stanislas Idzikowski. *A Manual of The Theory and Practice of Classical Theatrical Dancing*. (Cecchetti Method). London: Cyril Beaumont, 1971. (Orig. pub. 1922.)

Berger, John. *Selected Essays*, ed. Geoff Dyer. New York: Vintage International, Random House, 2001.

Blasis, Carlo. *The Code of Terpsichore*. London: Edward Bull, 1831.

Dowd, Irene. *Taking Root to Fly: Articles on Functional Anatomy*. Northampton, MA: Contact Editions, 1981.

Duncan, Isadora. *My Life*. New York: Liveright Publishing Corp., 1927.

Fitt, Sally, Dance Kinesiology. New York: Shirmer Books, 1988.

Fokine, Mihkail. Manifesto. *London Times*. 6 July 1914.

Franklin, Eric. "Dance Imagery for Technique and Performance." *Human Kinetics*, (1996), Champaign, IL.

Gardner, Howard. *Art Mind and Brain*. New York: Basic Books, 1982.

——— *Frames of Mind*. New York: Basic Books, 1983.

Ginsburg, Herbert, Sylvia Opper, *Piaget's Theory of Intellectual Development*. Englewood Cliffs, NJ: Prentice Hall, 1979.

Greenough, William. Report for the Proceedings of the *National Academy of Science*, 1990

Gregory, John. *The Legat Saga*. London: Javog Publishing Associates, 1992.

Haskell, Arnold. *Ballet Russe*. London: Weidenfeld and Nicholson, 1968.

Koegler, Horst, *The Concise Oxford Dictionary of Ballet*. New York: Oxford University Press, 1977.

Koch, Liz. *The Psoas Book*. Felton, CA: Guinea Pig Publications, 1997.

Kostravitskaya, Vera. *School of Classical Dance*. John Barker, trans. Moscow: Progress Publishers, 1978.

——— *101 Classical Lessons*. New York: John Barker Publication, 1979.

Kotulak, Ronald. Exercise builds up brain, studies show. *Chicago Tribune*, Sept. 2, 1990, 5.

Kuchera, Michael. *Postural Considerations in the Sagittal Plane*. Foundations for Osteopathic Medicine. Antioch, CA: Williams & Wilkins, 1997.

Lawson, Joan. *A History of Ballet and its Makers*. London: Dance Books, 1973.

Lee, Carol. *Ballet in Western Culture*. Boston: Allyn and Bacon, 1999.

Lewis, Daniel. *The Illustrated Dance Technique of Jose Limon*. New York: Harper & Row, 1984.

Makarova, Natalia. *A Dance Autobiography*. New York: Alfred A. Knopf, 1979.

Miller, Patricia. *Theories of Developmental Psychology*. New York: W. H. Freeman, 1983.

Noverre, Jean George. *Lettres sur la Danse*. C. W. Beaumont, trans. John Barker, trans. Dance Horizons, 1975.

Olsen, Andrea. *Body Stories*. New York: Station Hill Press, 1991.

Paskevska, Anna. *Both Sides of the Mirror*. New York: Dance Horizons, 1981.

——— 2nd edition. Princeton, NJ: Princeton Books, 1992.

——— *From the First Plié to Mastery*. Princeton, NJ: Princeton Books, 1990

——— 2nd edition, New York: Routledge, 2002

Paxton, Steve. "Still Moving." *Contact Quarterly*, Volume 3, Source Book. Special Edition. Northampton, MA, 1977–1978.

——— *Contact Quarterly*, Volume 7 1981–1982.

Piaget, Jean. *The Growth of Logical Thinking from Childhood to Adolescence*. A. Parsons, S. Seagrin, trans. New York: Basic Books, 1958.

——— *The Essential Piaget*. Howard Gruber, and Jacques Voniche, eds. New York: Basic Books, 1977.

Smith-Autard, Jacqueline M. *The Art of Dance in Education*. London: A&C Black, 2002.

Suzuki, Daisetz. *The Awakening of Zen*. Boulder CO: Prajna Press, 1980.

Sweigart, Lulu. *Human Movement Potential*. New York: Harper & Row, 1974.

Todd, Mabel Ellsworth. *The Hidden You*. New York: Exposition Press,1953.

Vygotsky, Lev. *Mind in Society, The Development of Higher Psychological Processes*. Cambridge, MA: Harvard University Press, 1978.

Ward Warren, Gretchen. *Classical Ballet Technique*. Tampa: University of South Florida Press, 1989.

Zelanski, Paul, and Fisher, Mary Pat. *The Art of Seeing*. Englewood Cliffs, NJ: Prentice Hall, 1988.

INDEX